D1027852

A CONVERSATION PIECE

Poetry and Art

Edited by
Adrian Rice and Angela Reid

The National Museums and Galleries of Northern Ireland
in association with
Abbey Press

Published by the National Museums & Galleries of Northern Ireland
in association with Abbey Press, Newry

A CIP record for this book is available from the British Library

Museums & Galleries of Northern Ireland Publication Number 4

ISBN 0 900761 42 3 *paperback*
       0 900761 43 1 *hardback*

Designed by Adrian Rice
Typesetting by David Anderson in 11/14pt Sabon
Printed in Northern Ireland by Nicholson & Bass Ltd

Cover Illustration:
John Walker, *Touch* (1970) © John Walker 2002,
Collection Ulster Museum, Belfast

**JENKINS
SHIPPING CO. LTD.**

NICHOLSON
& BASS LTD

CONTENTS

ABOUT THE SPONSOR

Jenkins Shipping Co. Ltd, the generous sponsor of this publication, has expanded its forward thinking approach to business to include patronage of the arts.

Historically based in Warrenpoint, the company has recently extended its operation to the port of Belfast, where its customers include some of the world's leading forestry product carriers and producers. The expansion to Belfast "was a natural progression", according to Walter Jenkins and "is in keeping with the company's commitment to provide the shipping industry with the quality of service it has come to expect from Jenkins".

Given the international nature of Jenkins Shipping's business, the expansion to Belfast is at a fortuitous time, as the city prepares to bid for European City of Culture in 2008.

Without the commitment of Jenkins Shipping Co. Ltd and its close co-operation with both Margaret Elliott, Chairman of MAGNI, and Michael Houlihan, Chief Executive of MAGNI, this collection for a new era might not exist. Sincere thanks are duly recorded for their enthusiasm, dedication, imagination and belief in this liaison of poetry, art and business.

Angela Reid
Co-editor

FOREWORD

The arts are our maps to the landscapes of the imagination, and through painting and poetry we share in the creative vision that is an essential element of the human experience. The National Museums and Galleries of Northern Ireland hold important collections of fine art, including, at the Ulster Museum, a notable collection of Irish art, tracing its development over a period of more than three centuries. Inviting poets – renowned for their abilities to weave cloaks of dreams – to respond in words to the art of the past is a wonderful way of using these collections as powerhouses of inspiration, and it is a delight to welcome the celebration of the creative spirit that has resulted from this unique collaboration.

Michael Houlihan
Chief Executive
The National Museums and Galleries of Northern Ireland

INTRODUCTION

Having had my own poems first published alongside artworks in the *Muck Island* (1990) box, in collaboration with Ulster artist, Ross Wilson, the idea that poetry and art are productive bedfellows has always seemed completely natural to me. So, when my co-editor Angela Reid – the book's originator – first asked me if Abbey Press might be interested in co-publishing a combination of poetry and art, I had no hesitation in recommending the idea to other members of the Abbey Press board. Being honoured by such an approach, my colleagues were easily persuaded to embrace what is now our fourteenth publication in just over four years, and it is one of which we are especially proud.

The National Museums and Galleries of Northern Ireland (MAGNI) house significant collections of fine art. One of the most important collections contains paintings and sculptures by Irish artists dating from the late seventeenth century to the present day. This collection was celebrated by the Ulster Museum in 1999 in a landmark exhibition entitled, *A Land of Heart's Desire: 300 Years of Irish Art*. Although the paintings on display during the exhibition provided the initial art hoard for this project (in which selected poets were invited to pick paintings on which to base new poems), Angela Reid and I quickly widened the poets' choices to include all available MAGNI artworks. Therefore, if they desired, the poets were able to look beyond the Irish collection for inspiration and into other collections containing works by several distinguished British and Continental Old Masters. Similarly, despite the temptation to canvass only Irish-born poets for the project, we decided that such a policy was unnecessarily restrictive. Although the vast majority of poets presented are Irish – from the north, south, east and west – the inclusion of several British and American voices undoubtedly enriches the mix.

Why *fifty* artworks and *fifty* poems? Simply, because we wanted to reproduce as many images as possible, allied to a wide variety of poetic voices. Concerning selection of the latter, we turned our back on any elitist agenda, preferring instead to include promising newcomers alongside recently established poets, school syllabus stalwarts and major poetry prizewinners.

It has been fascinating to see the different ways in which the poets have reacted to the challenge of this project. Having examined a particular poet's work, we then sent reproductions of certain images, one of which we hoped might spur the poet into verse. It was soon clear that some Belfast-based poets, like Michael Longley, had a working knowledge of the MAGNI collections, and joyfully seized the chance to pen an overdue homage to a cherished painting. On the other hand, many poets had no hard and fast idea of what they wanted and requested as wide a choice as possible, while a few others took up the challenge of responding to a narrow choice, of just one or two images. Then there were instances in which the twinning of poem and image seemed distinctly predestined: Ian Duhig's inventive interpretation of Sampson Towgood Roch(e)'s *Rustics Dancing outside an Inn* or Paul Muldoon's subtle sonnet on Anthony Green's *The Second Marriage*, spring readily to mind. And then there is the indefatigable Brendan Kennelly. A constant encourager, Brendan enjoyed the exercise so much that he submitted two different poems inspired by the same image. (We have included the second poem as an appendix.)

Overall, while some poets tackled quite abstract images, the majority were drawn to figurative works and landscape scenes. Regarding the popularity of individual artists, it is good to see the likes of Colin Middleton come to the fore, and slightly surprising to note the relative under-representation of the literary Jack B. Yeats. Nevertheless, the poets' penchant for poetic imagery is ably demonstrated in the strong showing of poet-painter George 'Æ' Russell.

As with any project of this nature, there are fortuitous spin-offs. For example, by choosing to write on Sir John Lavery's *Eileen, Her First Communion*, Sinéad Morrissey discovered the previously elusive and perfect cover image for her latest poetry collection. Moreover, several poets, who had been labouring through a lean spell, were openly grateful for having been prompted into writing again. And there lies one of the principal strengths of a venture like this: that artworks can be such a ready-made and profitable creative stimulus for a poet. Indeed, every contributor chose an image that, to put it bluntly, got them writing – which meant, in some cases, forsaking a coveted image that had turned out less amenable to their muse. The chosen artworks all offered up useful visual subject matter and suggestive themes, often influencing the very style and syntactical structure of the poems. However, I believe that the poems produced go beyond being slavish word imitations. They come across, rather, as protean echoes of the artists' painterly way of saying; echoes with minds of their own; echoes that do not just mimic but dare to talk back. As a result, an exciting two-way conversation has taken place – à la the book's title – between two historically affable art forms, in which the poet is no mere somnambulant illustrator of the artist's original work. Perhaps Aleksander Wat's poem, 'Facing Bonnard', best captures the essence of this artistic exchange. Translated by Czeslaw Milosz and included in his international anthology of poetry, *A Book of Luminous Things* (1996), the poem ends:

That translation from our world, don't ask whether faithful,
gives pleasure to the eye. The other senses are mum.
But to the eye it gives pleasure. That's enough. Quite.
Be patient. Wait. You will see how that pleasure
opens up as an egg of dream-meditation.
Our artist enclosed in it a ballet of possibilities
where he himself – and you – are both an observer and an author,
a corps de ballet, surely, but also a true soloist.

I would like to think that in this book the poets have engaged with the artworks and their given 'ballet of possibilities', while managing to remain, like the artists, 'true soloists' in their own right.

While the vast majority of the poems were specially commissioned, the knowledgeable reader will notice the inclusion of a few poems – including my own – previously published elsewhere. Basically, certain poets were keen to support the project by sending in a new poem. On reflection, however, they felt that one of their existent poems linked to a MAGNI artwork couldn't really be bettered. For instance, Seamus Heaney told me he wrote 'The Guttural Muse' following a night's fishing with the artist Barrie Cooke at the very place that inspired Cooke to paint *Big Tench Lake*. So Seamus duly nominated the painting as his chosen image and submitted the poem with the irresistible slogan, "… it's not new. But it's right."

With fifty artworks and fifty poets involved, it's not easy bringing a project of such scale to completion. Not surprisingly, much help was needed. Therefore, Angela Reid and I would like to thank the following: Michael Houlihan, Chief Executive, MAGNI; Margaret Elliott, Chairman, MAGNI; the sponsors, Jenkins Shipping (Warrenpoint) and Nicholson & Bass Ltd (Mallusk); Don Hawthorn, David Anderson and Robert South from Nicholson & Bass Ltd; Mel McMahon, Dermot McGovern, Patrick Mooney and Pat Crawley from Abbey Press; Elizabeth McWatters; Desmond Reid; Rosemary Stewart; Heather Henning; Michael A. Kinsella; and Molly Freeman, for her tireless secretarial support.

Finally, I want to refer to our choice of cover image. From a personal point of view, John Walker's painting *Touch* (1970) has a touch of destiny to it. Let me explain. Despite its Troubles notoriety, I enjoyed growing up in Rathcoole, north of Belfast. For one thing, you had plenty of mates to knock about with. And in such a huge housing estate you had lots of scope, not just for mischief, but also for games of all kinds, especially for football, whether it was matches held on dark winter nights with garage doors for nets or summertime kickabouts on the grass pitch at Derry Hill. And then the immediate environs were not bad either. Within minutes you could be building huts on Carnmoney Hill; or mucking about at Hazelbank on the shores of Belfast Lough; or roaming around Belfast Zoo and Bellevue Amusements under the shadow of Cave Hill. Now this was all very well for a 'wee' lad. However, as a grammar school kid, still sport mad but with a growing interest in books and music, you sought stimulus outside the estate, travelling with your mates in a double-decker bus or a black taxi to Belfast. And one of the places, which provided that stimulation, was the Ulster Museum.

I have to confess that two of the Museum's greatest attractions were its free admission (thankfully still in place) and its Café (even with the sobering graveyard vista, a kind of *carpe diem* admonition to our youthful waywardness). But the Museum's exhibits were also of interest to us, particularly those found in the art galleries. We saw much to admire there, although admittedly sometimes the artworks on display, especially those of an abstract nature, were the focus of our attempts at Pythonesque humour. We would sit opposite them and try to guess their titles or, knowing the titles, we would rename the works altogether. The results were side-splitting. Looking back now, I can acknowledge the childishness and philistinism of such behaviour. Yet, I also believe our irreverence signalled a healthy scepticism, indicating that we were beginning to think for ourselves.

But here's the point: John Walker's *Touch* was *the* artwork at the centre of our tongue-in-cheek renaming game. Big and bold, a deliberate fusion of the abstract and the figurative, *Touch* is the kind of painting that people either like or loathe. With peer group pressure then holding sway, we (pre)tended to favour the latter. We had innumerable alternative and unflattering titles for *Touch*. Two that stick with me are 'Luminous Lollies' and 'Double Lollies, Green Period', both of which likened the two green objects in the painting to a popular type of hard sherbet lollipop still available in corner shops today. But now, at last, I can admit that the painting did secretly impress me, and continues to do so. Furthermore, it is amazing to realise that out of the many wraparound cover images considered for this book, *Touch*, the teenage 'conversation piece', works best. I trust that both it, and more importantly, the dialogue between poetry and art that it encloses, will give the reader much cause for thought and talk.

Adrian Rice
Jordanstown
March 2002

Ut pictura poesis

(In poetry, as in painting)

HORACE

ON THROUGH THE SILENT LANDS

Jack Butler Yeats

ON

Lord why did you plant me in dreamtime
and then let me melt?
why did you say
this is a pierless bridge you're travelling
that ends in space ocean air
it's that little matchstick trestle
in *On Through the Silent Lands*
– the rawpaint plain
river
and haunted pilgrim

he's slinking down from the mountain
an old man in a dark suit
that's as shiny as an elbow patch
– he clutches a bowler hat
as though he's a tired member
of some ruined L.O.L.
a brother who's walked away from the Field
so many long miles
he holds his bowler sadly
as you might a book or a satchel
maybe his sword lies broken
in some birdless corrie
or behind a betting-shop
on the Ormeau Road?
let's call him Dick
Mr Richard Crossan
an outofwork actor
or a bankrupt pigfarmer
walking down towards the bridge

not the dream of becoming
nor the dream of belonging
but the dream of Being

Tom Paulin

THE POTATO DIGGER

Paul Henry

THE SOLITARY DIGGER

for Sister Anna Danaher

Not a spire in sight but thatch and hay.
She pauses from her digging. All alone
She digs out good potatoes from the clay.
She'll fear no winter when the work is done.
The crop is good. She pauses for a rest –
No famine now will skeleton the land;
A simple faith submits that God knows best –
There are things she knows she needn't understand.
Just a simple peasant standing with her spade,
Knowing through her hands the fertile earth
In a landscape with not a tree for shade –
This land is hers by labour and by birth.
She pauses from her digging; there is time
To compose oneself where heaven and nature rhyme.

Gabriel Fitzmaurice

BEWLEY'S RESTAURANT II

Hector McDonnell

QUITTING THE BARS

Quitting's hard but staying sober's harder.
The day by day; the drudge and boredom bit;
not sure if the self is cell or warder.

You quit the bars; you quit the sordid ardour;
you quit the tulpas sucking on your tit.
Quitting's hard but staying sober's harder.

You sometimes think you got away with murder.
The shady souls regard you as you sit –
you wonder if they are wards or warders

in this sad café. The mind's last border
dissolves. Guilt has done a midnight flit.
Quitting's hard but staying sober's harder.

So sip cool water; the light's a wonder
streaming out in wave-particles. You've lit
up bright your prison cell. Body – warder

of your dreams – will be the dreams' recorder,
though wrapped still in a coat that used to fit.
Quitting's hard but staying sober's harder;
stranger for your being both ward and warder.

Paula Meehan

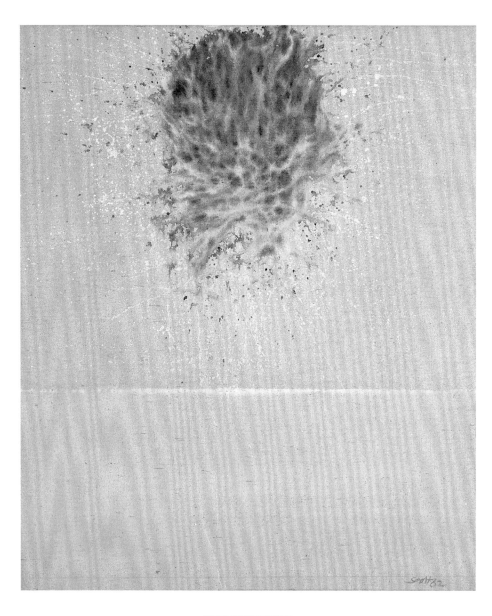

YELLOW DEVICE

Patrick Scott

VARIATIONS ON YELLOW

Sun brushes the mountain
before landing on a field
    so lush with buttercups
    they might yield
a painter's yellow pigment
or be cultivated as a cash crop.

◆

    The swelling yellow sun of early May lures you
westwards again: a country bolt-hole, weekend hideout,
lakeside shack, some perch you can escape to,
    draw back creaking shutters, air out dusty rooms.

◆

The relief when a cloud,
    eclipsing the sun, steps out of the light
and fishermen in yellow oilskins
    glisten like the yolk of a guillemot's egg.
A kittiwake takes the plunge, snatches
    a slapstick fish clear of the waves.
It's anyone's guess what may happen next.

◆

You want to stay for as long as this
yellow painting radiates illumination,
the way someone in a lunch break
music shop hesitates to walk out
on a mezzo in full flight: you'd like
that light to shadow you down
the street, pursue you to your desk.

Dennis O'Driscoll

THE ROAD TO THE WEST

John Luke

THE ROAD TO THE WEST

I prefer the road west.
Once you collide with
the coast of the Atlantic
you've got decisions to make.

Will it be rowboat,
multi-hull catamaran
or luxury liner
on the searoad west?

Don't rule out hot air balloon
or submersible – these options
can turn a junket
into an adventure.

Me – I take the sky highway
for westward wanderings.
What can refresh, I ask,
like a pre-moistened towelette?

Floating through cloud corridors
cocooned in cotton puffs,
you are so above it all.
I admit it *can* be a bumpy road

what with headwinds and turbulence
and how you're surrounded
by air everywhere:
I arrive home at the hour I left

but closer to the west.

Julie O'Callaghan

YELLOW BUNGALOW

Gerard Dillon

YELLOW BUNGALOW

A reproduction of your *Yellow Bungalow*
Hangs in our newfangled kitchen, dream-mirror,
A woman waiting between turf-box and window
For a young man to put away his accordian
And gut five anonymous fish for supper.

She appreciates the disposition of skillet
And kettle on the stove-top, of poker and tongs,
And keeps her distance in her faraway corner
Beside the Atlantic, while he has learned new tunes
And wants to accompany us to another room.

As soon as I've switched the fan-assisted oven on
And opened the bombinating refrigerator
(I've a meal to prepare) I hear bellows wheeze
And fingernails clitter over buttons and keys.
Cooking smells become part of the composition.

Michael Longley

VIEW OF PONT AVEN

Roderic O'Conor

PAINTER AT WORK

You have been painting all night.
A sea has rushed through your head,
dragged you way down under an idea
that must roll its way into your evening.
You have felt it would come all day –
your eyes glazing over when others spoke,
your distracted reach for a brush
you picked up, then put down,
the time not right just yet.

In your flat, your door firmly closes
and the light under the gap is sharp, says go away!
People come and go. The chicken is roasted and eaten.
Cigarette smoke asks after you.
In your absence we play your music –
find in your notebooks only scribbles where once you sketched,
hear through the wall nothing,
though your open-laced boots flung on the floor, your jacket
slouched on the door knob tell us that you're still there.

The ending is always quiet.
A picture fills a space and is with you everywhere –
balances over the kitchen work-top where you scoop
muesli into your dazed morning mouth, is hung
just above bath water where you soak for ages,
unsettles the dust we forgot was thick on our bedside table,
is high ahead of you down streets to your studio –
your city becoming its rhythm
until at last you are satisfied.

You come home and this painting is a gift –
a bright sea-view when someone is feeling low,
a vast landscape to arrive at when others gave up hope.
The hard work over, you can
talk freely of your day now,
mix olives with feta cheese and greens,
raise your glass, your lips,
your eyes, your heart,
to the life
that will be painted about again.

Enda Wyley

RIVETERS

Cloth-capped and in the street clothes that had been
A Sunday best for bandstands in the park,
The ship's side sheer above them, new-milled steel.

That blessed moment which all art imposes ...
Before the war, before the Troubles, or
Before our ma died and we went to granny's.

A disappointment to the puzzled Left,
The workers of the world once burdened with
Dreams born amid the bourgeois biedermeyer
Or in the schoolyard as the hot tears started.
But – since it's Belfast – staunch and true defenders
Of privilege, religion, freedom, laws.

Good draughtsmanship recalls us to the facts.
They are using a pneumatic riveter.
One cracks a joke. The youngest's not amused.
Apprentices are usually the butt.
Men riveting. Men punching in the hours.
Men paying for hire purchase with their time.
Men taking some pride in a skill they've learned.
Not noble proletarians, nor even Prods,
Not working for the red dawn or the grey.
Not builders of the future, though the ship,
Titanic, towers above them, plates in place
For who knows what, torpedoes, icebergs or
Some profit to the owners, after which
The breakers would dismantle it again.
The plates go back into some mill and issue
As new Toyotas for their sons to buy ...

RIVETING

William Conor

He drew them walking home in '41
Or anyway away from work, perhaps
A cool, dark pub and ready for a pint.
A War Artist by then, he had to give it
A title that would justify the fee
Of fifty quid, so called it *The Home Front*.
And faith. *The Home Front*. It is always there.
Before and after war and revolution
Though king or country may not greatly care.

Anthony Cronin

GIVE ME TO DRINK

Colin Middleton

GIVE ME TO DRINK

There is nowhere for me
But the unwelcome house of this sixth man,
His wife speechless and infirm.
Get to Jacob's well. He does not even
Speak my name. His head swollen with araq
Confounding clarity, air listening fearful
Between lemon tree and almond.

Get to the well. And the stranger there
Like a bird with a damaged wing:
Give me to drink.
I am become a donkey drudging
For all mankind.

He is a Jewish prophet.
I am a woman of Samaria:
My bent shoulders, my beaten back,
Bare breasts, big rough hands,
How can everlasting enter me?

The stranger knew about the five husbands.
I needed him to say, All old
Old men. The first, sobbing his own dry lack,
Sending me to my father a barren woman.
Their rigid bones, dying skin, their grunts,

Hungry ghosts in sleep
Dragging them to ground,
Keeping me to serve till death.
I know that what one soweth
Another reapeth.

The stranger reads the flesh on my cheek bones,
Mortification on my lips. Is stern.
I see distorted in his eyes my naked nipples
And the starving, drifting end of him.

Joan Newmann

SLAN LEAT A ATHAIR / GOODBYE, FATHER

Séan Keating

JAMES JOYCE ON INISHERE

You might not notice him at first,
the solid-built man in the cloth cap
at the heart of the exchange.
Good shape to him, carpenter's shoulders,
years away at the building, home
a few years by the easy stance, his money made.
Clean white shirt under the sweater.

He's watching a man who's away himself, the sea calling him,
another man on the oars already, a third ready to shove off.
The last handshake for the priest, farewell
to native pieties, to neighbours and friends;
the priest's brother stands solid on the earth
and our Jim is there as the rest, indifferent to exile,
trusting that each must master his fate. The eyes

have a distance of their own. Other seas there, and skies,
a broader compass he knows in his bones;
the roundshouldered priest will not meet his look.
We imagine long winter nights, the one bowed down
with weariness of sin and the world, the other remorseless,
unblinking behind stone walls, under low skies.

Do they walk by the sea, we wonder, these island solitaries,
one going north, the other south, salute without speaking?
Does each have the other's measure, does anyone else know
their eternal war, monotonous as the sea's growl and rumble?
One keeps the ledger of an absent god, writes out the law;
One has the modest loneliness of Lucifer.

Theo Dorgan

EILEEN, HER FIRST COMMUNION

Sir John Lavery

EILEEN

Years later, after the painting, we planned her wedding.
The dress took days. We cleared the parlour floor
and flooded it with fine, ivory material.
Eileen disappeared. We worked steadily,

stepping carefully over the borders
her body would fill. On the third day my sister
and I raised a dress in her absence
that made her terrified. Too similar,

was all she said. Was it the weight,
we wondered? The colour? But she was back
with the old panic, her desperate familiar.
When the hour came she walked straight

past the saints and up to the altar
without glancing back. Childhood
had turned her neck towards us, once.
At eighteen resolution didn't falter.

Sinéad Morrissey

FARM IN WINTER

Tony O'Malley

NADIR

Then the last luminaries went underground.
The sea expressed its characteristic view
With long, hard sighs, raked echoes from the strand.
Someone pressed at the window to remark
Spring's white-wash on the shit-house good as new.
There was smoke but no fire. There was almost no smoke.
But these would later come into their own,
The luminaries said; as sure as corn
In August, as the rising of the lark,
They'd wet the baby's head, declare it sound
And send it on, green-lit, to Tyrone.

Carol Rumens

MR. AND MRS. STANLEY JOSCELYNE: THE SECOND MARRIAGE

Anthony Green

MR AND MRS STANLEY JOSCELYNE:
THE SECOND MARRIAGE

Standing as they do, all primped, primed, pukka, all proper, all property-lined, in a room
where every rift's loaded with ore,
they're reminiscent less of a blushing bride and a nervous groom
than a pair of con artists summoned before
a magistrate inclined to throw
the book at con artists so that, despite his efforts to sustain
the argument that, as distinct from his previous situation in Rugby Row,
everything here hinges on his shadow meeting her shadow-stain
on the carpet, it looks very much as if, for Mr Stanley Joscelyne and his mate,
the case will turn
rather on the provenance of a single inanimate
object – that silver cigarette-urn,
it would appear, set on the occasional table
in the centre of the room – and the outcome is, as he himself would put it, "inevitable".

Paul Muldoon

ECCLESIASTICAL RUINS ON INNISCALTRA

Bartholomew Colles Watkins

RUINS OF HOLY ISLAND ON LOUGH DERG

'I could eat you,' he said.
　　She replied that only lovers and cannibals talk like that.
　　　　(Sean O'Faolain, *Lovers of the Lake*)

No, not that Lough Derg, the other. Not where your mother,
aged sixteen, did pilgrim circuits on bare feet
until they bled. She bussed back to the farm in early dawn.
Excited, pure OK, but starving after three days' fast –
and still no food, till twelve that night –
and could smell from three miles off
her mother frying scallions. Pearls she couldn't eat.
That pilgrimage, and others (Lourdes, Knock),
made her what she was, upholder of the rosary
in Battersea. But she never forgot that sweet-
stink breakfast fry-up. Renunciation. Having to be good.

This painting is another holy island, the ski-run
lake we saw, shining by the fountaining apple-tree
at your ex-garden's end in Killaloe. A teenage paradise.
You wanted, then, to stay for ever. All these years,
and love's as delicate as Ming calligraphy. We slip among
the eighteen moons of Saturn in each other, role-
playing father, mother, holy island, child. *Hold
me – I'm in ruins. Golden apples. Roots. You're all I need.
Drink the water. Get more sleep. Trust me – I'm always here.*
Whatever you yearned for as a rolling-eyed blonde kid
is part of me. Like this lake with island, ruby hills and tower,

as gazed at from the real estate
your dad invested in to lure her back
to what he ached for after thirty years away. His earth,
his patch of Galway sky. Damned if she would. Lough Derg?
God no. It was years – five years – before she'd go.

Behind that brick-blown ruin, the painter's done
a sunset of goodbye. The isles of not just Galway – Greece,
before it could be free. Everything, except the gold light,
gone. Streaks of cloud reflected in the lake, as pink-
glass as the pendant hung in her corsage for nights
at the Irish Club. As backdrop, the soft, translucent gray-
blue-yellow of prawn-tails in Galway's Sushi Bar. *Raw fish?*
How things had changed by the time your dad and mum
came back. I wish I'd known her, wish she could have tried –
but by then she couldn't eat sugar – the Easter almond-cakes
I bought for her, from Crete. I wish

they hadn't waited, in London's shadow
of shelved objects, to go home. That her flood-tide
of prayer had worked. Will it work for us? As the sun-dial
moves through afternoon, I wish I didn't feel this putting off
(when can we live, and sleep the night – wild, side by side
and rain-drop tender, honest, calm – together without harm
to anyone?) is waiting for a wishbone, wishing on a jack-
knife moon. Like that pared flick in the painter's goldwash air:
stained, where it bellies to the lake, like coral lip-stick.
Like the coral you say she wore to match her hair. Still flame,
still sunset-bright, that one year home they had before he died.

Ruth Padel

CLAOCHLÓ

Tá mé ag ullmhú le bheith i mo chrann
agus chan de bharr go bhfuil dia ar bith
'mo sheilg gan trua; é sa tóir orm go teann;
mé ag éalú óna chaithréim spéire, mo chroí ag rith
ina sceith sceoine roimh bhuile a dhúile.

D'aonghnó tiocfaidh claochló aoibhinn ar mo chló.
As mo cholainn daonna dhéanfar stoc darach.
Tiontóidh craiceann ina choirt chranrach; gan stró
athróidh an sruth fola ina shú, an gheir ina smúsach.
Fásfaidh duilleoga ar mo ghéaga cnámhacha.

Cheana féin tá mo chuid ladhra ag síneadh,
ag géagú amach ina bhfréamhacha féitheogacha
ag buanú sa chréafóg; ag taisceadh is ag teannadh.
Mothaím mé féin ag imeacht le craobhacha
nuair a shéideann bogleoithne fríd mo ghéaga.

Inniu chan ag análú atá mé ach ag siosarnach
agus mé i mo sheasamh caoldíreach gan bogadh;
éanacha na spéire ag ceiliúr ionam go haerach.
As an tsolas diamhair seo atá mo spreagadh
go dil, cruthóidh mé clóraifil, mo ghlasdán.

Cathal Ó Searcaigh

FIVE TREES BY A RIVER

Hans Iten

TRANSFIGURED

I am getting ready to become a tree,
not because some god is after me,
bearing down with his aerial authority,
my heart bolting from the thrust of his need.

My figure will be transfigured, in one go;
my human shell turned to the trunk of an oak,
my skin twisted to gnarled bark, my blood-flow
to sap. Out of my branch-bones leaves will grow.

Already, my fingers and toes are stretching out,
elongating into sinewy roots,
tucking themselves tightly into the ground;
and when a breeze blows my branches round,
I feel as if I'm going nuts, or out

of my tree. Today I stand tall and straight,
not breathing but rustling; birds congregate
in me, warbling airs while I create
chlorophyll, inspired by unfathomable light
to fulfil my destiny, synthesize my fate.

Cathal Ó Searcaigh
(translated by Frank Sewell)

EVENTIDE

George William 'Æ' Russell

THE TURNING

They pause in the turning of the evening,
words surfacing like fish come up to feed.
When the story's shared, they'll leave
the shelter of the broken wall
to make for home, crossing bare brown bog,
bunching long skirts, balancing baskets;
finding their way
through tussocks of purple heather.

Another time they'll come, ready
for confidences, for warm twilight air,
for the white wing of a gull
crying overhead. But that time
might be lacerated by wind and driving rain,
hooded with heavy shawls that never part.

No, this is the evening they will remember,
back in the house with the fire to tend,
the husband hungry and the children wild:

the prop of the wall against their hips,
their elbows resting on cosy wicker rims,
the nearness and stillness of the water,
how the sky spread around them
in layers of lavender and turquoise;
and their voices lingered
like the light of the risen moon,
touching stone
before the vast swallow
of the dark.

Katie Donovan

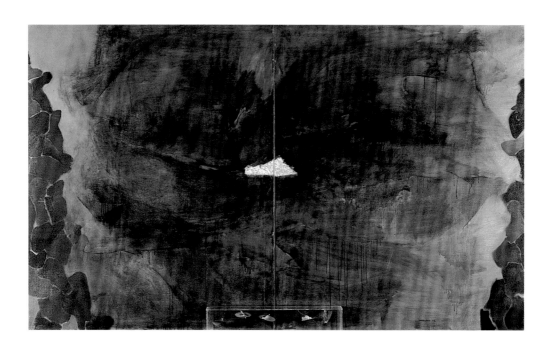

BIG TENCH LAKE

Barrie Cooke

THE GUTTURAL MUSE

Late summer, and at midnight
I smelt the heat of the day:
At my window over the hotel car park
I breathed the muddied night airs off the lake
And watched a young crowd leave the discotheque.

Their voices rose up thick and comforting
As oily bubbles the feeding tench sent up
That evening at dusk – the slimy tench
Once called the 'doctor fish' because his slime
Was said to heal the wounds of fish that touched it.

A girl in a white dress
Was being courted out among the cars:
As her voice swarmed and puddled into laughs
I felt like some old pike all badged with sores
Wanting to swim in touch with soft-mouthed life.

Seamus Heaney

GIRL IN WHITE

Louis le Brocquy

THE GINGER JAR

No matter how long and hard
This GI bride

Stares past the ginger-jar
Into the empty air

And the clouds of dust
Her ceiling lost

In last night's raid,
Along the Antrim road

There will still be people
Buried under rubble

And the bombers will return
Wing upon wing,

Whether the porcelain urn
Is T'ang or Ming.

Martin Mooney

INSIDE No. 3

Robert Ballagh

INSIDE

It's classic yours truly:
all winter spent moaning
for sunlight, all summer
confined to the bunker.
Instead of the shade
of a billowing whatsitsname,
it's cheeseplants and curtains
and Boredom City, Arizona,
like a tone of blue
that kind of hurts
and goes on kind of hurting
so as to seem to say
'This ain't gonna stop'
and not even a vision
of your sweet self, sugar,
on the spiral stair
in your birthday suit
will alter it one jot.
Is any of this getting through?
Let's face it – coming to
to the usual décor
and putting up the sneakers
and taking in muggins here
jawing away on the box,
the remote in one paw,
a Harp in the other,
the mute button activated
– what else is there?
Fresh air? Nature?
The great outdoors? Oh, sure.

Conor O'Callaghan

FIELD OF CORN, PONT AVEN

Roderic O'Conor

EN PLEIN AIR

Six weeks on a student exchange in Pont Aven
arranged by friends of my sister's au pair's friends
which landed me right in a bristling divorce,
and a set of parents, fixed and furious.
The village was *gentil*, its views inbuilt
on cornfields and their spontaneous gilt
that came to its own conclusions in the high
ambitions of a couple of cypress boughs.
He'd leave the house at 6 a.m. and come in
at midnight to the bed-settee turned down.
She chain-smoked and took to sleeping late
in a fug of insults I never could translate
while their troublesome daughter had an exchange
of her own with a decorator from Limoges.

Artichokes, *Orangina*, tarte tatin,
a third-hand collection of French reggae bands.
The chic sister up from Paris at weekends,
the lads on mopeds that dropped her home again
in the small hours. Inspector Clouseau on TV,
laughed at by no one in the room but me.
Chantal's friends, bikini-d and sunkissed,
me in a black one-piece with a padded bust
and freckles and my one practised French phrase.
Occasionally, the rows would get too crazed
which were the times I'd light out on my own,
with my phrasebook tucked up high under my arm,
calling through the closed doors on my way,
'*Maintenant, je vais me promener*'.

Vona Groarke

JOHN MONTAGUE

Edward McGuire

THE YACHTSMAN'S JACKET
a portrait of Edward McGuire, RHA

Eddie, old friend, gone to the shades,
we both walked a while on the wild side.
You endeared yourself to me first
as you swayed above your father's swimming pool
and proclaimed: 'Let's have a piss!'

Two golden arcs in the Blackrock night.
Viking berserk, your drinking bouts:
wrecking Garech Browne's tiny mews flat
in a fracas with Dominic Behan,
angry, after you had upended Kathleen.

And I was crashing a party in Sandymount
when you came hurtling, backwards, out;
you stopped to say, 'Hello, John', then
lowered your head to charge in again,
waving your weapon, a bottle of stout.

Your humour as wayward as your anger.
Standing beside Barrie Cooke in P. Pye's flat
when Barrie, per usual, rippled a fart,
you unfolded your lean height, to declare:
'Picasso, perhaps, but a scruffy painter from Clare

has no right to poison my air.'
Behind all the rattle, awkwardly shy,
the unhealed hurt of a mother's boy,
all that lostness wrought to tension, fury
of contemplation, schemes of colour harmony,

the sitter's face, the leaf at the window.
Your Freudian trademark; that spiky dead bird.
Though you were gentle as you were wild,
charting the glooms of our middle-class Bohemia,
but also tender portraits of a girl child.

In due course, I joined your gallery,
to be received with old world courtesy,
before we clambered to your studio:
the draped camera, plus the green visor
to enable you to concentrate on your task.

It was rainy and cold when I left,
so you settled your sailor's jacket
over my shoulders. 'I won't need it,'
you expostulate gently. Its bulk protects
me still, as I trudge fields of West Cork.

John Montague

REQUIEM
for Ann Maguire

Do you remember the day
You drove me round Fermanagh
Filling me full of histories
I didn't know
Amongst the legendary
Woods and lakes and all those
Holy places
Your passionate commitment
Was more holy than the stones

Do you remember that day
Spent in the family farmhouse
Stout as a fortress
You gave off to your kid brother
Like a mother.

Do you remember
Looking for that pub, we couldn't find
But you always remembered.

Do you remember
Way up on Sligo's coast
In the mizzle, beside
A heaving sea
We walked, underneath a shared coat
Laughing at history's quirky reversals.

Look! Look!
In the tumult of the waves
Two dolphins rise and fall and are
Swallowed up in the sea
While we, stand
Timorous, sheltering,
Wanting to ask questions
Maybe to touch and crush away
A strange distance!

CHILDREN PLAYING ON LAGAN

Gerard Dillon

In that church, as they spoke of you
I shuddered
Like so many men, unmanned and weeping.
When they put you in the ground
I could not believe
In the earth's warm embrace
I choked,
My throat was full
Like a corn-filled pigeon

Driving around your townland
For hours,
I tried to remember all of it
And find an answer for my anger
I listened to the radio
Somewhere in its electrical ether
Nat King Cole was singing
Strongly resonant out in the wet lushness
Of Fermanagh.
Then it came to me,
Releasing me,
Everyone in the cemeteries
Held one another
Touched, embraced
Received the vital need of one another
Wordlessly

In that rain-filled moment
I heard a murmur of birdsong
Low and melodious
A soft elegy, enfolding us all

I remember still those swimming fish
Oblivious to the seas turbulence
I'll go looking for them again
If distance, time or tide
Prevent me,
I'll find you
Amongst the wood pigeons.

Brian Keenan

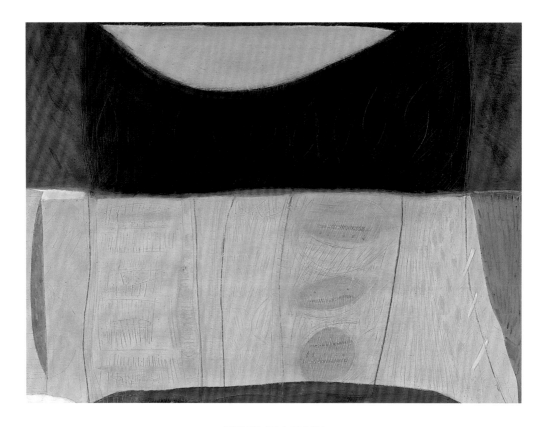

GHOST OF A PLACE

Tony O'Malley

THE IVY ROOM
in memoriam Hubert Butler

The inches and ha-ha. Somewhere out of view
The last shimmy of the canal essing
Towards Bennettsbridge. Inside the Bernouilli Effect
Took little draught-sips out of the open sash

Like eddies at the edge of the Nore. It was all
Bareness and fresh paint and Shaker geometries
Of light on the varnished knots and dark varnish of pineboards
Burnished with use. Where Butler wrote, the shelves

Emptied of *The Bell* but carrying, like this,
The ghost-ivy of lives. All at once I was back
To the Sufi house near Stolac: the sheer karst
Rising a thousand metres, the blue calligraphy of swallows,

Gushing subterranean river a Balkan jade. Brilliant fountain
Light of St John of the Cross flowing miles
Out of its mountain dark to the small wooden window
In a bare white prayer room furnished with kelims

And spared the infernal cleansing. A single vocable
In green Arabic on the limewash of the walled river garden
Shaded by pomegranates. In the sash's distance
The round tower of Tullaherin and, invisible under Mt Leinster,

The hamlet of Graiguenamanagh. Now forsythia and Scullabogue
Were blossoming in Kosova, a spring bonfire was a Shiva raging
In the walled garden. Small still point of the Ivy Room
In a lea of history. A sickle on whitewash. Zen in Kilkenny.

Chris Agee

THE FUN OF THE FAIR

A. Romilly Fedden

WHERE UNCLE WHEN
in memoriam William Bond

Where, uncle, when, your hands touch
my windowsill-sitting days

– as much light and shadow at play
as in Tex Ritter movies –

will you be drawn from long pockets,
silences and loose change,

and led too slowly to the fair,
where the magical air takes *whoop*

or *look no hands,* when I'm leaning far out
of the saddle waving in winds where

the splashed crowd melts in the spume's revolve around
the humping-back horse skewered by golden thread to the ground.

Where, uncle, when, the clown's tent is raised
still find me running, flat-out, full of praise

on the yo-yo and swizz of poetry,
where the grazing horse gilts,

and at high noon or night, shadowless feet
don't touch the ground.

John Brown

DAYLIGHT RAID FROM MY STUDIO WINDOW, 7 JULY 1917

Sir John Lavery

DAYLIGHT RAID FROM
MY STUDIO WINDOW,
7 JULY 1917

What fowl are these, flown home to roost? The sky
eye-bright and bird-shot, the window rippling
and gaping, black-out blanked out, dawn peeling
back its speckled shell, the air droning: I
forget where I am – Cromwell Street, London
vanish into colour and its plots. White
muslin bleaching stiff in a bleaching frame.

And she so like a swan, you'd mistake her
for Pavlova from afar, her linens
feathery, organdie stiff-starched, muslin
layer on layer laid thick as down. And her feet
dangling languorous, ruddering, urging
her upward, her shoulders arched, wings in flight –
ever that girlish posture, in dismay

or delight. Spoiled meat, gutter crumbs, bruised fruit
scrubbed in public fountains – the past so vast,
the present so unlikely, I forget
what's in the wind. Cromwell Street, a window
thrice a wife's height, fires over London
where one leads one's double life. So much to
keep her in linen, keep her linens white.

And she so like a swan, I forget where
I stand, my brushes heavy with the vast
and open air, a fallen sister or
madonna painted out, in, out again –
colour and its plots, that look of terror,
all of it visionary, sky-blown. Once
a woman – what woman? – lifted, kissed me.

Nathalie F. Anderson

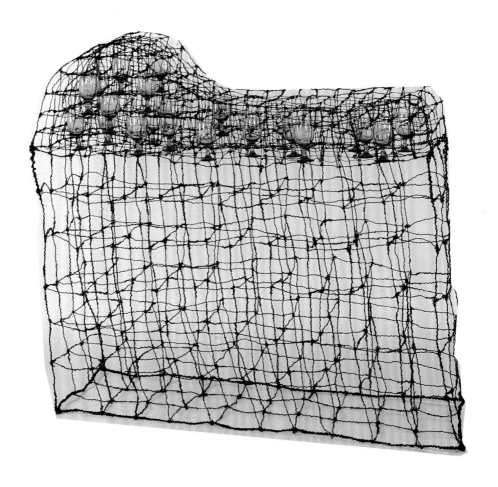

PASSION BED

Dorothy Cross

PASSION BED

A new geography: how
lately I have begun to travel your body
with a kind of carelessness, knowing
the journey is repeatable,

to look at you without hurry
knowing you'll be there
at the end of it, the rainbow
at the end of the rainbow, gently

persisting.
Intently, then, we burrow into one another
and come back whole, to the calm night, fur
in our mouths, bone on the tongue, resting.

Peter Sirr

HEAD

Colin Middleton

THE MASON'S TONGUE

Although a likeable, charitable soul,
He had a less than secret tongue;
So it was removed, and entombed
A ritual distance from the shore –
Sealed dumb in the packed sand.

When a young man dug it up
(Out toiling for some bait)
It dropped from the wet spade
On to the cool slab of strand,
And lay like an odd curl of meat.

The young man cupped it in his hands
To get a closer look,
When, stirring on his palms
And with a strangely mournful note,
It suddenly began to speak:

Go tell all the brethren
There is no rest where I have gone,
No answer comes from Jah-Bul-On.

Bewildered, and seized with sudden dread,
He let the tongue flop to the sand,
Then scooped it back up with his spade
And flung it out across the waves.
Yet, though hushed upon the ocean bed,
The tongue's words lapped about his head:

Go tell all the brethren
There is no rest where I have gone,
No answer comes from Jah-Bul-On.

Adrian Rice

THE WATCHER

George William 'Æ' Russell

THE WATCHER

What are we to do with those
whose death was not an ending?
Who could not say what they meant.
Who did not know what they felt.
Their faces fill the rivers,
their need darkens the fields.

When you, say, wash up, take one
of their hands inside your own.
Smooth some liquid, thick and green,
over finger, wrist and palm.
Let your hand feel an oily glove
dissolve in warm water.

Find a spoon. Hold it until
all is a spoon's shape and weight.
The light locked in soap suds
will be there when each has burst.
Dry your hand with that light,
the ordinary light of day.

Mark Roper

DAWN, KILLARY HARBOUR

Paul Henry

KILLARY HARBOUR VIEW
Map L Grid Ref. 897625

Painter, would you have me sit
before Dawn's worn, faded vestment?
Would you have me at the edge there
leap, and fall headlong into it?

And in falling for dear life, in hope,
would you have me cling to the folds
of holiness, all frayed and tarnished,
like one in search of guiding stopes?

In broad daylight, when things are clearer
and there's nothing like an evanescence
or revelation, forgive me painter
if, with compass, map and heavy boots

I revisit the cold and dark of water's depth,
the roughness in the grits and quartz.
Though I can almost touch the purpley veil
you've draped across slopes, sea and sky,

carefully, I wipe your vision from my eyes.

Edward Denniston

RUSTICS DANCING OUTSIDE AN INN

Sampson Towgood Roch(e)

WATERCOLOUR

for Elio Cruz

Scorpions rule the sand once Babylon: a spider binds
Kubla's bones; God is dead; the French are on the sea
and in his whitewashed Bath atelier Sampson Towgood Roch(e)
finishes the picture and the picture inside the picture
commissioned to the title *Rustics Dancing outside an Inn*
(a tight blue jacket bellowing 'Jolly! Got that? Jolly!').
He steps back. No one will really look at it anyway.
They'll glimpse a new daub hanging over the damp patch.
Jolly. But there's more here they'd think worth hanging.
In its distance, a neurasthenic Anglican cathedral
steams through the gathering waves of the countryside.
Edging round one corner of the Spa House Inn, a tree
menaces some baked hedgehogs cooling on the porch roof.
Hope and Charity are mob-capped concierges at the door;
at the window, Faith is over a barrel. Chickens fly past.
A shadowy fiddler can't watch his fiddle's scroll uncurl,
proving itself possessed by Babylonian incubus Pazzuzu.
Right, her bustle the size and shape of mainland China,
Harpo's nurse ignores his hand become a scorpion's claw.
Beyond them, Screaming Lord Sutch pours Death a double
cream. Soon they'll reel about like cows. Opposite,
the dancing couple. He's as smug as buttered parsnips
despite entertaining scarlatina and an eerie crotch,
and fancies himself a Burke to her Marie-Antoinette.
Yet she is brightness of brightness, her brow without flaw
under a bonnet nodding towards Donatello's brave David.
But look closer. There is no sense of freedom in her steps.
Consider too the blood-red rosebud mouth, breast implants
and Chinese bound feet. She only smiles down on her apron
to show solidarity with continental Masonic radicalism.
Her hourglass figure is set to swell and burst its stays,
to gush wave upon tidal wave of sand, creating a desert
blank and pitiless, boundless and bare of this city awash
with watery people of watery taste drinking watery tea;
this waste of pastel stucco, this snotty, Godforsaken Bath!
Sampson Towgood Roch(e) laughs to himself, silently, forever.

Ian Duhig

TIRED CHILD

Louis le Brocquy

TIRED CHILD

Pin-wheel spins
As his hot breath blows
I, like a baby,
Can do nothing but gasp

Merry-go-round turns
As his hard arm throws
I, just a child,
Can do nothing but grasp

I cannot breathe
He will not stop
You laugh
You laugh

Molly Freeman

THE THREE DANCERS

John Luke

THE THREE DANCERS

You stirred imagination
into the swirl of golds and olives,
terra-cotta, azurite and pearl –
the adamantine mix
your steady hand produced
to grace your northern landscape
with a sweep of sylvan forms
from Arcady.

Entranced,
drawn out of your head,
dancing across the canvas
leap by measured leap,
their gesturing limbs
describe nothing
of a Dionysian cult,
no tearing flesh.

All familiar landmarks
every corner, every crookedness
contoured to a curve.
Without blurring your vision
you carefully draped the ground
to take these steps, distinct as birdsong
garlanding earth and air
in a different light.

These are your butterflies,
these are your gentled hills.
This is a land not lived in
but desired.

Ruth Carr

DREAM OF THE MOTH

Colin Middleton

DREAM OF THE MOTH

As though she has become the negative's print,
She leaves behind her silhouette, her trace;
Has the grub spewed her? Do we see a hint
Of chagrin on his neanderthal face?

She walks on air, a tentative toe in light,
Like all young women coming to the world
For love; her apprehension shows she might
Find where love lies waiting, dormant, furled.

And when she finds it she'll become the moth,
Flitting through night, whirling around the flames
Of things unspeakable. Her turquoise cloth's
Already bursting, ripe for passion's games.

The painter knows a leaf looks like a heart,
In red and blue and gold, a map of veins;
He also knows this child will soon be part
Of love's experience, those fantastic pains,

That drive us underground, searching for hope,
For warmth, for pleasure – anything to hold
Our future, or a means to help us cope
Before we sink to earth, as leaf to mould.

Frank Delaney

THE POTATO GATHERERS

George William 'Æ' Russell

THE POTATO GATHERERS

They know what they're doing at the worst of times,
these three unpraying desperadoes
on home ground. No time to notice
the sun's orange angelus at their backs,
any more than we, halfway back to them,
paused for the cold shine in October skies
when the digger clattered past, anointing us
with wormly wet earth and withered-white
potato-plant pipes as we clutched for the seed,
for cold gold in the seam of gutter.
In that impressionist twilight, you can't make out
their fingers: even their bent backs you'd see better
with our millennial 20-20 sight
from a west-bound jet over Belmullet.

Bernard O'Donoghue

SHAPES AND SHADOWS

William Scott

SHAPES AND SHADOWS

The kitchens would grow bright
in blue frames; outside, still
harbour and silent cottages
from a time of shortages,
shapes deft and tranquil,
black kettle and black pot.

Too much the known structures
those simple manufactures,
communion of frying pans,
skinny beans and spoons,
colander and fish-slice
in a polished interior space.

But tension of hand and heart
abstracted the growing art
to a dissonant design
and a fat dream of paint,
on the grim basic plan
a thick white pigment

knifed and scrubbed, in one
corner a boiling brown
agony of mahogany,
behind which there loom
ghosts of colour and form,
furniture, function, body –

as if to announce the death
of preconception and myth
and start again on the fresh
first morning of the world
with snow, ash, whitewash,
limestone, mother-of-pearl,

top-of-the-milk cream,
bleach, paper, soap and foam,
to find in the nitty-gritty
of surfaces and utensils
the shadow of a presence,
a long-sought community.

Derek Mahon

HAZEL LAVERY, THE GREEN COAT, 1926

Agreed image, of your open self, your personhood,
do not put me into a sadness like your own,
though I am using your heated body with its
easy mark of beauty, its narrow grip on a segment
of the abstract world, for some clues.

He has been able to bring your inner sun
to full view, a real heartbeat and a lucid mind
inhabiting a body degrading into matter:
like a rosary made of plum stones, built en
colombage, your hospitality towards death

is the light of my own country. The lamp
without oil in your spine, a hand-made candle
to light me to bed. Your sense of chastity
starts a shape in me attached to life at all
four corners, saying what your beauty means to you.

A wave heaping itself to feast like a plant
on much of what flames in my eyes, the world
of speech, a world that seems bared of its covering,
and has not a bone in its body. You are walking
within a tulip, and a fire of sea-coal in your house,

not yet numbered, leaves a blue path through
the warm cinder of your head. You throw a veil
of sinewy deception, of half-grown leaves,
over your eyes, walking up Air Street that moon-
ark body you had so often laid down.

So that the living seem to go to bed
with the dead, most seasonably, a boy hobbles
with a log at his foot to kiss the bell-handle
of your lodgings: his most used words inking
that wintry mantle of aged snow, floating

THE GREEN COAT

Sir John Lavery

in the middle of the unstitched page. You have
what used to be called a military bearing,
which is that of a child asleep on a cross,
the whitish patina of verdigris and rose
carmethian that begging soldiers forge

on the eight hanging days, as their ivory ticket
to the damaged sky where heaven tries to see itself.
And it is as though you actually wore armour,
with nineteen horses killed under you, seated upon clouds,
your seas unsailed since his blood fell directly

into the unfixed horizon.

Medbh McGuckian

VILLAGE BY THE SEA

Norah McGuinness

VILLAGE BY THE SEA

It can't be Ireland. There's not enough green.
The foliage is chartreuse or aquamarine
or indigo. Those ochreous pillars vacillate …
twin yews, golden and fastigiate?
Or rowing boats propped up against a wall …?
And why are the people so tall?
They'd surely have to bow their heads to grace
the interior of that Georgian farmhouse
which, spliced to the sympathetically lit church,
is the centre of gravity of this painting-cum-parish.
Beyond, the landscape, becoming primitive,
casts its questionable sense of perspective
to the wind: over the cliffs of clay,
raw and sheer, into the incoming bay
above which, this extraordinary village is
(look at the lean on the fishermen's cottages!)
teetering – unstable as a poem –
but loved (one imagines) and home
to the lady in red and the lady in black
who've met at the bend. Later, walking back,
they'll meet again and feign surprise and say,
all pleasantries exhausted, 'That's the way'.

Jean Bleakney

DUBLIN STREET SCENE NO. 1

Edward Burra

DESIGNING FRIDAY

At the Corner of Talkers
a man with his back to the wall
thinks he knows the story behind the hoofers
this Friday. Hot secrets under her shawl
let crafty knackers think they know
of the love Batt Shanahan going blind
heaps on her and she takes with few
words. 'Batt', she said once, 'love is a sound,
listen for it.'

Fierce common sense, her own kind
of pride, trot with her and Diarmuid
past the Corner of Talkers. She sees everything,
lets on to see nothing, scours shops, finds
what she wants, drinks two creamy pints, hears
sounds not love, shawls homewards, designing,

leaving windows and walls to do the watching, listening.

Brendan Kennelly

BOON COMPANIONS

Harry Kernoff

BOON COMPANIONS

for John Coyle

You can see them still, shadows
of the men my father might have met
sixty long years ago among the snug
and smoky parlours of Dublin pubs.

He chose not to. Other servants,
civil or not, of the state they were in
found solace, chance companions
and some cheer amid the porter,

players and punning of these palaces
of wisdom, but he dutifully came home
from a day and often a night ministering
to justice, murmuring to my mother

of Mr Aiken, Mr Traynor and Mr Berry,
of border manoeuvres and Dail debates
that sometimes went on far too long
and saw us safely to our early sleep.

I think of him often, but I think, too,
of these men, these straitened toffs,
sardonic artists, irresolute rebels
and treasonable clerks, their holy hours

bonded by ash and booze and badinage,
and wonder what failure of nerve or hope
led them to this kindness of strangers,
this fleeting comfort, and wonder also

why I, who never was my father's son,
am so anxious for their casual approval
and hanker to sidle up to them and say:
so, gentlemen, and what is it you're having?

John Boland

FÊTE DAY IN A CIDER ORCHARD, NORMANDY

William John Hennessy

A THANKSGIVING

As she thinks of his caress
she pushes tears from her eyes
and cries, 'Bad cess
to him' and 'Why's
there always such a price
to pay for happiness?'

Her sorrow and to spare.
'It was a thing of nothing,'
she heard him declare.
Until it grew.

Some said
that's the way it ever was.
He takes what he wants,
and she's left with
what she doesn't.

◆

Married, and not for love.
Everybody knew.
And knew
that's why
he withdrew
and came back in a uniform.
But what could you
rely on? A game-bird not to stray
or lay among long grasses
and the roots of vines?

As the children lay
untroubled by their futures
at a thanksgiving in Normandy
one evening when the rain
held off
she found among the shades
and fallen leaves a windfall –
and she rose
out of the dark of mercy
into its day.

Peter Fallon

NEGATIVE (4)

Dearly beloved,
I take tonight as my text
the remorseless morse, the randomness
(not knowing where the next
move's coming from –
not knowing
which quarter of the human,
or the animal kingdom
the next move's coming from)
seemingly evinced in this jam-
jar of unseemly frog-spawn.

It has stood still,
dustily simmering with a Brownian motion
on the high-up, distant window-sill
of my upbringing
(the big wide wonderful world
beyond the glazing, then
the big wide wonderful world
beyond the glazing, hi!)
until, on a day of shimmering rain,
it has come to me, as in, as in a dream …

I was parked in Park Street,
outside, as was my habit, Barney Dunne's
with abject Missouris
pouring down the windscreen,
to the dashboard – *O me miserum* –
each chasing another's tail,
each following its own destiny,
each catching up, each swallowing,
each being itself, at last, swallowed,
when through this diagrammatic rain

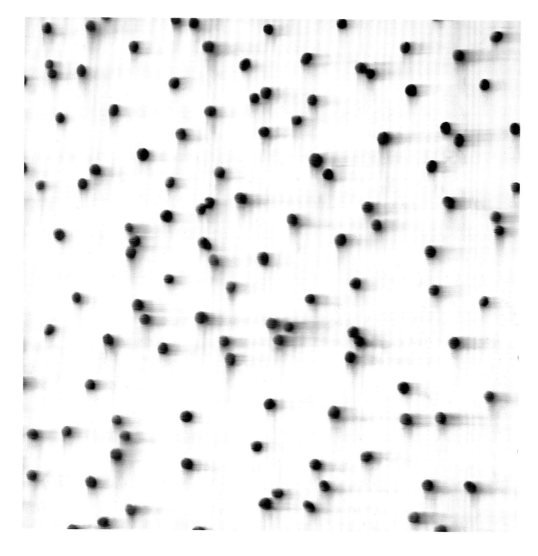

NEGATIVE (4)

Mark Francis

a diagram appeared:
nine burnt-out matchsticks
that floated in outer space
and formed a tortoise or *testudo*:
and a voice that, in the circumstances,
must needs have been St Bernard's of Clairveaux,
who spoke from between my shoulder-blades.
'God,' the voice said,
'and this is the long and the short of it –
is simply the length and the width
and the depth and height of it, lo ...'

Leon McAuley

HUCKLEBERRY FINN

Aloysius O'Kelly

HUCK FINN

This could be heaven –
Standing at the water's edge
Enjoying the summer's appetite
For shadows, sunshine and peace –

But beneath you, small fish flicker
And your rod, unnoticed, bends
Under the weight of your reflection
Tugging for release.

Mel McMahon

THE BARN (BLUE II)

Basil Blackshaw

JIMBO BLUE

Jimbo Blue come blow your horn
The barn is far afield.
The crow's wings are on your head
The hounds are at your heels.

The turtles' feet about your neck
Drip with water deep.
The wild waves that lash the deck
Have lulled you half asleep.

Black Elk dances the dance of death,
'It is a good day to die.'
Buffalo, bear, and deer descend
Into the darkening sky.

Lightening Hopkins howls the blues
Wailing through the night.
Conrad dreams deep Congo drums
Thundering skins drawn tight.

The boards they bend about to break
White horses foam at mouth.
The doors are open wide awake
The bow heads farther south.

The skull upon your wizened rod
The gems that are its eyes
The teeth through which the winds bite
Bright beads are tears it cries.

Jimbo Blue come blow your horn
The barn is far afield.
The crow's wings are on your head
The hounds are at your heels.

Rand Brandes

THE FOX

John Luke

THE FOX

I am stepping out to meet you
From this crazy world he has made.

Just think, for a minute,
That when I hit the floor before you

The hair will stand at the back of your neck;
The attendant who knows me

Only too well, or the lady who allowed
All this to take place,

Will turn, shocked, when I shake
Myself, and the voluptuous scene,

With those birds, whatever they are,
And burst through the clouds of your living room

Or the abstract museum,
And make everything happen

For real this time.

Gerald Dawe

SCENE IN CO. WICKLOW

James Arthur O'Connor

GONE

Arriving in darkness
to faint cries from the dock,
silhouettes working the guyropes

and grab, no one coming ashore
and gone before morning;
and as it goes the picture

composed by your window
over the harbour reduced
to a ship pulling out, drawing

the tide behind it
and as you watch, become
indistinguishable in the distance,

where it will stay, unseen
but in place, forever.

David Wheatley

LAGAN: ANNADALE, OCTOBER

Colin Middleton

LAGAN, ANNADALE

There is something about this side of the river
that is the right side to be on. You know the trees
are set to survive the war, those walkers face
steadily into their lives, that child, you trust,
will grow to take peace for granted.

Praise to the enduring present, its gift today
a cocky tugboat puttering towards Drumbo,
or its home wharf, or autumn's furthest edge.
It holds the centre. Gracing its advance,
the wake fans out, lapping both banks at once.

Frank Ormsby

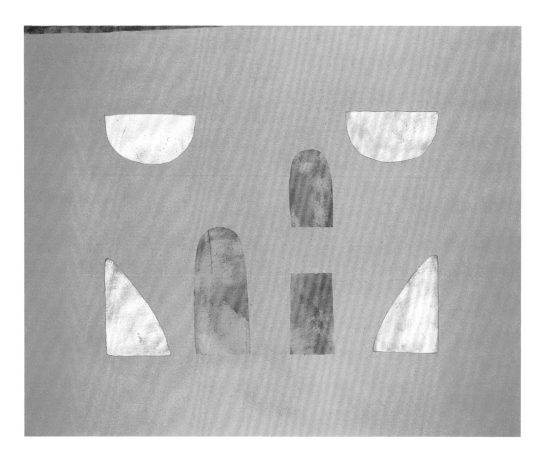

EGYPT SERIES No. 3

William Scott

SPACED SHAPES
IN A SPACE OF SAND

The sands
an ochre stretch
giving nothing, being only
themselves.

The shapes
lying over these sands,
making space
in the space
for red doorways
out of nowhere
leading only
to a fade
of silence broken
by the low drone
of white buttresses
scraped onto red
to hold back the sands
and let the bowls give
with abundance unhampered
by introspection,
though it's clear
that the scoop on the left
knows
whence it came ...

It's wonderful, this stuff,
from a hand that once recorded
harbours, slagheaps, Breton landscapes,
tables cluttered with veg and delph.
So it's okay to be sparse,
to lose sequence and belonging;
under all our plots
this vast, clean silence.

Kerry Hardie

THE END OF THE WORLD

Jack Butler Yeats

APOCALYPTIC

It moves as it is drawn by the future tense: a flexed wave
That talks like a crowd with a rumour of quarrels,
Piles over a reef of glossaries.

Withdrawing, it sucks away pebbles, rattling, dumping
On open mouths, boulders flattening words.
So the words are there, but stopped. When the wave returns

It will flow over all the names
And the macaronic street cries,
Put out the watchman's brazier.

Words will be there but already
Written in the new cursive
They appear like flourishes at the edge of a tide,

A repeating film and ripple of wavelet
That covers bright sand with a blade clear as ice.
The weights are buried.

The voice of the wave will be all
We will be expected to understand.

Eiléan Ní Chuilleanáin

THREE FRIENDS

Daniel O'Neill

LOST

Three days since the boat's come,
the weather worsening by the hour.
Last month it was three weeks –
the helicopter brought medicines,
stale loaves, tins of spam.

A gull bent-backed in the wind,
getting nowhere. Mundy's bin
tossing on the waves. The electricity wires
taut as fiddle strings, loosing
their own ghostly music.

Where are the crows that sit on them?
And where are the artists to paint all this?
They come like tourists
when the weather's fine, taking
whatever we have.

The last corncrake I saw
went away in a painting.
So did my three-legged dog.
And, after they were painted with me,
my two friends went to the mainland.

What kept me behind?
Well, they sneaked out on me
while I slept off a siege of drink.
They were shits, surely,
but the painting made them that way.

I see the three of us again
on that canvas, the sunlight
only on me. No wonder
they changed. And my eyes
looking nowhere, already lost.

Matthew Sweeney

SELF-CONTAINED FLAT

Gerard Dillon

WISH YOU WERE HERE

I'm sending this postcard not from somewhere
Exotic, but from the middle of my life
(It's useful, once in a while, to take stock),
And, as you can see, the head's above water,
The wolf absent from the door. It's shocking though,
How fragile all this seems sometimes – contingent
On so many things, or so few, it makes me dizzy.
This morning I was planting cherry trees,
Turning the earth with an old Lurgan spade,
And I thought of that last summer in Belfast
All those years ago and miles away –
Remember? The early heat, the blossom everywhere?
You were so full of youth it hurts me even now
To recall the lustre of your skin, its radiance.
Without knowing, I think I've missed you ever since.
Send all the news you have. Send a picture.

Kevin Smith

APPENDIX

('Herself and Himself' is Brendan Kennelly's alternative –
and equally entertaining – poem also inspired by Edward
Burra's *Dublin Street Scene No. 1*)

HERSELF AND HIMSELF

They're driving in
from the cricketing fields of Dublin
past the Five Lamps, Empress Lane
and the Corner of the Talkers
where you'll still get wind
of the bombing of the North Strand
in a war we were no part of
or so we thought. It isn't always
we know what wars we're in.

There's shopping to be done,
young mouths waiting for baker's bread.
She knows the shops, the men and women
behind the counters. She knows himself too.
On a tough journey, a few words will do
to ensure the future will be fed.
She does the shops, gets what she wants,
they have two creamy pints together
then hit for home
between the worked fields and the sea,
herself and himself
words and silence
peace and war
you and me.

Brendan Kennelly

NOTES ON POETS

Chris Agee grew up in Massachusetts, New York and Rhode Island. Since 1979, he has lived in Ireland. *First Light*, shortlisted for the 2000 National Poetry Series in the US, will be published by the Dedalus Press, Dublin, in 2003. His previous volumes of poetry are *In the New Hampshire Woods* (The Dedalus Press, 1992) and a chapbook, *The Sierra de Zacatecas* (Ediciones Papeles Privados, Mexico City, 1995). A collection of Balkan essays, *Journey to Bosnia*, will appear in 2002. A former editor of *Poetry Ireland Review* and *Metre*, he edited a Special Double Issue on Contemporary Irish Poetry for *Poetry* (Chicago, Oct-Nov, 1995), and an anthology *Scar on the Stone*: *Contemporary Poetry from Bosnia* (Bloodaxe Books, 1998). A selection of his poetry is included in the forthcoming historical and contemporary anthology, *The Book of Irish American Poetry* (University of Notre Dame, 2003). He teaches at the Open University in Ireland and edits *Irish Pages*, a journal of contemporary writing based at The Linen Hall Library, Belfast.

Nathalie F. Anderson is a Professor of English Literature and Director of the Programme in Creative Writing at Swarthmore College in Pennsylvania, where her teaching includes courses in Contemporary Irish Poetry. Her first collection of poems, *Following Fred Astaire*, was the 1998 winner of the Washington Prize awarded by The Word Works, a small press in Washington DC. Nathalie Anderson's poems have appeared in such journals as *Prairie Schooner, Southern Poetry Review, Madison Review, Nimrod, Spazio Humano* and *Paris Review*. She was the librettist for the opera *The Black Swan*, based on Thomas Mann's novella *Die Betrogene* – a collaboration with the composer Thomas Whitman which premiered in the fall of 1998 in a production directed by Sarah Caldwell. Nathalie Anderson was a fellow at Yaddo in 1986, and in 1993 was awarded a Pew Fellowship in the Arts.

Jean Bleakney was born in Newry in 1956. A former biochemist, she currently works in a garden centre. She joined The Queen's University Writers' Group in 1993 and was a runner-up in the 1997 Patrick Kavanagh Poetry Award. Her first collection was *The Ripple Tank Experiment* (Lagan Press, 1999). Subsequently, she has received awards from Belfast City Council and The Arts Council of Northern Ireland. A second collection, *Synchronous Gardenias*, is due in 2003. She lives in Belfast with her husband and two children.

John Boland lives in Dublin, where he was born. He is a critic, lecturer and broadcaster and was named Arts Journalist of the Year in the 1998 ESB National Media Awards. His first full poetry collection, *Brow Head*, was published by Abbey Press in 1999.

Rand Brandes teaches English and Creative Writing at Lenoir-Rhyne College in Hickory, North Carolina. A Fullbright Fellow and an active critic, he has published articles on Seamus Heaney, Ciaran Carson, and Medbh McGuckian among others. His first book of poems, *Balefires,* was published in 1997 by White Fields Press, Louisville, Kentucky.

John Brown studied English Literature and History at Bristol University and Scottish Literature and History at Edinburgh University. He co-edited *Gown Literary Supplement* in Belfast in the 1980s and has regularly contributed poems to journals, magazines and books in Ireland. He currently works as Literary Arts Officer with the Arts Council of Northern Ireland.

Ruth Carr, formerly Hooley, was born in Belfast in 1953. She edited *The Female Line* (1985), an anthology of poetry and fiction by Northern Irish women writers, and is currently associate editor of *HU* poetry magazine. A founder member of the Word of Mouth poetry collective, she works as a tutor in adult education and her first collection, *There is a House*, was published by Summer Palace Press (1999).

Anthony Cronin is a comic novelist, broadcaster and poet. He has published several books of poetry, including *New and Selected Poems* (Raven/Carcanet). He has been editor of a number of literary publications, received awards for his services to Irish literature, was cultural advisor to the Taosieach and responsible for establishing Aosdána, an Irish state body that funds writers. Among his prose works are *The Life of Riley* and *Dead as Doornails* and two celebrated biographies of Flann O'Brien and Samuel Beckett.

Gerald Dawe was born in Belfast in 1952. He now lives in Dublin where he teaches at Trinity College. His most recent collections of poetry are *Heart of Hearts* (1995) and *The Morning Train* (1999). *Stray Dogs and Dark Horses*, a volume of selected essays, was published in 2000 by Abbey Press.

Frank Delaney is a novelist and broadcaster, who was born in Tipperary in 1942. After an early career in banking, he joined RTE in Dublin as a newscaster and programme maker and then transferred to the BBC as a current affairs reporter, eventually moving into arts broadcasting.

Edward Denniston was born in Longford in 1956. He attended Trinity College Dublin and now lives in Waterford, where he teaches English and Drama. His first collection, *The Point of Singing*, was published by Abbey Press in 1999.

Katie Donovan was born in 1962 and spent her youth on a farm near Camolin in County Wexford. She studied at Trinity College Dublin and at the University of California at Berkeley. She lives in Dublin where she is a journalist with *The Irish Times*. Her first collection of poetry, *Watermelon Man* (Bloodaxe Books) was published in 1993. Her second, *Entering the Mare*, was published in 1997, also with Bloodaxe. Her third, *Day of the Dead*, will be published in 2002. She is co-editor, with Brendan Kennelly and A. Norman Jeffares, of the anthology, *Ireland's Women: Writings Past and Present* (Gill and Macmillan, Ireland; Kyle Cathie, UK, 1994; Norton & Norton, US, 1996). She is the author of *Irish Women Writers: Marginalised by*

Whom? (Raven Arts Press, 1988, 1991). With Brendan Kennelly, she is the co-editor of *Dublines* (Bloodaxe, 1996), an anthology of writings about Dublin. Her poems have appeared in numerous periodicals and anthologies in Ireland, the UK and the US. She has given readings of her work in many venues in Ireland, England, Belgium, Denmark, Portugal, the US and Canada. Her short fiction has appeared in *The Sunday Tribune* and *STET* magazine. She is currently writing a novel.

Theo Dorgan is a poet, radio and television broadcaster and scriptwriter. He recently retired from his post as Director of Poetry Ireland/Éigse Éireann. He has published three books of poetry, *The Ordinary House of Love* and *Rosa Mundi*, both from Salmon Publishing, and *Sappho's Daughter*, from Wave Train Press. He is the editor of *Irish Poetry Since Kavanagh* (Four Courts Press), co-editor of *Revising the Rising* (Field Day) and of *The Great Book of Ireland*. A selected poems in Italian, *La Casa Ai Margini Del Mundo*, was published by Moby Dick, Faenza, and *Sappho's Daughter* in Spanish translation is due from Ediciones Hiperíon, Madrid. He is a member of Aosdána.

Ian Duhig has received Arts Council and Cholmondeley Awards, won the National Poetry Competition twice and the Forward Tolman Cunard Prize. His most recent book is *Nominees* (Bloodaxe, 1998) and his next is forthcoming from Picador.

Peter Fallon has most recently published *The Deerfield Series: Strength of Heart* (1997) and *News of the World: Selected and New Poems* (1998). At the age of eighteen, in 1970, he founded The Gallery Press which he continues to edit and direct. Inaugural Heimbold Professor of Irish Studies at Villanova University, Pennsylvania, in the Spring of 2000, Peter Fallon lives with his family in Loughcrew in County Meath.

Gabriel Fitzmaurice was born in 1952, in Moyvane, County Kerry where he still lives. He teaches in the local National School. A former Chair and Literary Advisor of Writers' Week, Listowel, he is author of more than twenty books, including poetry in English and Irish, children's verse in English and Irish, translations from the Irish, essays, and collections of songs and ballads. An award winner in the Gerard Manley Hopkins Centenary Poetry Competition, he frequently broadcasts on RTE radio and television and local radio stations on education and the arts. His latest collection for adults is *A Wrenboy's Carnival: Poems 1980–2000*. His selected essays, *Kerry on my Mind: of Poets, Pedagogues and Place*, was published in June 1999.

Molly Freeman was born in Charlotte, North Carolina, in 1971. Her heritage is both Irish and Cherokee. She holds degrees in Theatre Arts Education and English as a Second Language. In America, she has worked extensively in the theatre as an actor, director and stage manager. She has also held various teaching positions in schools and colleges. Before coming to Northern Ireland, she was the Education Director of Hickory Community Theatre. Now living in Belfast, she works as a freelance artist in drama and creative writing and is on the NI Arts Council's 'Artists-in-Schools' scheme. She is currently co-writing a book with poet Adrian Rice that focuses on creative dramatics and creative writing projects for the classroom. Her poetry has been published in various US magazines and journals.

Vona Groarke was born in County Longford in 1964. Her first collection, *Shale* (The Gallery Press, 1994) won the Brendan Behan Memorial Award in 1995. Her second collection of poems, *Other People's Houses* was published in 1999 by The Gallery Press and was received by the *Times Literary Supplement* as a 'remarkable collection'. In that year also, she was guest editor of a special edition of the American poetry journal, *Verse*, on the subject of 'Women Irish Poets'. Her poems have been anthologised in *Making For Planet Alice* (Bloodaxe Poets, 1997) and *New Poetries* (Carcanet, 1996). She has been Writer-in-Residence with the National University of Ireland at Galway and at Maynooth, and with Cavan County Council. Recent prizes won include the Strokestown International Poetry Competition (1999), and the Stand International Poetry Competition (2000). Her third collection, *Flight*, was published this year by The Gallery Press.

Kerry Hardie was born in 1951. Winner of the PHRAS Open Poetry Competition 1997, the Friends Provident/National Poetry Competition, 1996, and a School of Irish Studies Foundation Award 1998. Joint winner of a Hennessy Award for Poetry. Pamphlet *In Sickness* published by the Honest Ulsterman, 1995. First collection, *A Furious Place* published by The Gallery Press, 1996; second collection, *Cry for the Hot Belly*, Gallery Press 2000; first novel, *Hannie Bennet's Winter Marriage*, Harper Collins 2000.

Seamus Heaney was born in County Derry. A resident of Dublin since 1976, he teaches regularly at Harvard University. *Death of a Naturalist*, his first book, appeared in 1966, and since then he has published poetry, criticism and translations which have established him as one of the leading poets of his generation. He has twice won The Whitbread Book of the Year, for *The Spirit Level* in 1996 and *Beowulf* in 1999, the latter translation being an international bestseller in 2000. In 1995, he was awarded The Nobel Prize for Literature. His eleventh collection, *Electric Light*, was published by Faber and Faber in 2001. His selected prose, *Finders Keepers*, was published by Faber this year.

Brian Keenan was born in Belfast in 1950. He took honours English at the University of Ulster and later completed an MA in Anglo-Irish Literature at the same university. He worked as a teacher and Community Development Worker in Belfast for seven years before going to teach in the American University Beirut, Lebanon. His publications include, *An Evil Cradling*, which won four national and international awards; *Between Extremes*, a best selling account of travels in Chile; and *Turlough*, a novel based on the life of Turlough O'Carolan.

Brendan Kennelly was born in 1936 in Ballylongford, County Kerry. He is Professor of Modern Literature at Trinity College, Dublin. He has written novels, plays, essays and several books of poetry. He achieved international recognition with his poetry epics *Cromwell* (1983) and *The Book of Judas* (1991). His most recent poetry publication is *Glimpses* (Bloodaxe, 2001).

Michael Longley was born in Belfast in 1939, and educated at the Royal Belfast Academical Institution and Trinity College, Dublin, where he read Classics. His collections include *Gorse Fires* (1991), which won the Whitbread Prize and *The Ghost Orchid*. His most recent collection *The Weather in Japan* (2000) won the Hawthornden Prize, the T.S. Eliot and the Irish Times Prize for Poetry. His *Selected Poems* was published in 1988. He has edited selections of the poems of Louis MacNeice and W.R. Rodgers. His anthology *20th Century Irish Poems* was published by Faber in March 2002. A Fellow of the Royal Society of Literature and a member of Aosdána, he was awarded the Queen's Gold Medal for Poetry in 2001. He and his wife, the critic Edna Longley, live and work in Belfast.

Derek Mahon was born in Belfast in 1941, studied at Trinity College, Dublin, and the Sorbonne, and has held journalistic and academic appointments in London and New York. A member of Aosdána, he has received numerous awards including the Irish Academy of Letters Award and the Scott Moncrieff Translation Prize. His *Collected Poems* was published by Gallery Press in 1999.

Leon McAuley was born in Dungannon in 1952, and brought up in the Glens of Antrim. He is the author of four books: *Veronica*, *The Fountain*, *The Right Log* and *Albert and the Magician*. He presents Radio Ulster's book programme, *You're Booked*.

Medbh McGuckian was born in Belfast in 1950. She met and was influenced by the 'Group' of Ulster poets at Queen's University. Her work has been published by Oxford University Press and later Gallery Press and Wake Forest Press in America. She has been Writer-in-Residence at most Irish Universities, now organising the new MA in Creative Writing at Queen's University, Belfast. *Shelmalier* was published in 1998.

Mel McMahon was born in Lurgan in 1968. His work has appeared in numerous books and journals, including *Signals: An Anthology of Poetry and Prose* (Abbey Press, 1997). He currently teaches and lives in Newry, County Down. His first chapbook of poems is due from Abbey Press in 2002.

Paula Meehan was born and lives in Dublin. Most recent publications are *Dharmakaya* from Carcanet Press, her fifth collection of poems which received the Denis Devlin Memorial Award, and *Cell* from New Island Press, a play, which was shortlisted for Best Play in the Irish Times Theatre Awards. She has worked with many visual artists including Marie Foley (*Six Sycamores*), Ita Kelly (*Mysteries of the Home*) and Eithne Jordan (*Desire/Pillow Talk*).

John Montague was born in Brooklyn, New York, in 1929, returning to his parents' native Ireland in 1933 where he grew up on the family farm in County Tyrone. He has produced a steady stream of publications – poetry, prose and literary criticism – including two long poems, *The Rough Field* (1972) and *The Dead Kingdom* (1982), the novella, *The Lost Notebook* (1987), *Born in Brooklyn* (selected writings, 1991), *Collected Poems* (1995), a short story collection *A Love Present* (1997) and *Smashing the Piano* (1999). He has recently published a memoir of his early life, *Company* (2001). Also an editor and critic, he produced the groundbreaking *The Faber Book of Irish Verse* (1974), and *The Figure in the Cave* (1989). In 1998, he was appointed the first occupant of the prestigious Ireland Chair of Poetry.

Martin Mooney was born in Belfast in 1964, and currently lives in Whitehead with his partner and their two children. His first collection, *Grub*, won the 1994 Brendan Behan Memorial Award. Mooney has published the pamphlets *Bonfire Makers* and *Operation Sandcastle*, as well as a second full-length collection *Rasputin and his Children* (2000). A volume of short stories is due for publication in 2003.

Sinéad Morrissey was the youngest ever recipient of the Patrick Kavanagh Award in 1990, when she was eighteen. She published her first collection *There Was Fire in Vancouver* in 1996. This collection was distinguished with an Eric Gregory Award by the London Society of Authors in the same year. In 1999, she was the recipient of a bursary from the Northern Ireland Arts Council, awarded as financial help towards the completion of her second book. Sinéad's work has been published widely in Ireland, the UK, New Zealand, Australia and the United States, and has appeared in four separate anthologies. Her second collection, *Between Here and There*, has just been published by Carcanet.

Paul Muldoon was born in County Armagh in 1951. He moved to the United States in 1987 and has held various university teaching posts, most recently Director of the Creative Writing Programme at Princeton University, where he is Howard G. B. Clark Professor in the Humanities. In 1999, he was elected Professor of Poetry at Oxford University. His most recent books are his translation, with Richard Martin, of *The Birds of Aristophanes*, and *To Ireland, I*, his 1998 Clarendon Lectures. His *Poems 1968–1998* was published by Faber and Faber in May 2001.

Joan Newmann knew Colin Middleton in the 1960s. She is a graduate of Queen's University. In 1965, her first chapbook, *First Letter Home*, was published by Queen's University Festival Publications and her first solo collection, *Coming of Age*, was published by Blackstaff Press in 1995. *Thin Ice*, a chapbook, was published by Abbey Press in 1998. A new collection of poetry is due in 2002. She lives in County Donegal.

Eiléan Ní Chuilleanáin was born in Cork in 1942. She is now a fellow of Trinity College, Dublin, and Associate Professor of English, as well as an editor of the literary magazine *Cyphers*, since 1975. Her latest book of poems is *The Brazen Serpent* (Dublin 1994, Wake Forest 1995). She has also published translations of poetry from Irish and other languages (most recently *The Water Horse* with Medbh McGuckian, from the Irish of Nuala Ní Dhomhnaill).

Cathal Ó Searcaigh is the author of eight collections of poetry. His work has been translated into twelve different languages. He is a member of Aosdána. Recently, he received an honorary doctorate in Celtic Studies from the National University of Ireland. His selected poems in Irish *1975–2000* have just been published. His next publication will be about his travels in Nepal.

Conor O'Callaghan was born in Newry, County Down, in 1968. His first collection of poems, *The History of Rain* (Gallery Press, 1993), won the Patrick Kavanagh Award in 1993 and was shortlisted for the Forward Best First Collection Prize in 1994. A second collection of poems, *Seatown*, appeared from Gallery Press in April 1999, and from Wake Forest University Press in the US in March 2000. He was Writer-in-Residence at UCD for 1999–2000, and was Writer-in-Residence for Dun Laoghaire/Rathdown in 2001. He reviews occasionally for the *TLS* and *Poetry Ireland Review*.

Julie O'Callaghan was born in Chicago in 1954, and has lived in Ireland since 1974. Her collections of poetry include *Edible Anecdotes* (Dolmen, 1983), a Poetry Book Society Recommendation, and *What's What* (Bloodaxe, 1991), a PBS Choice. Her latest collection, *No Can Do* (Bloodaxe, 2000), is a PBS Recommendation. Her books of poetry for older children include *Taking My Pen for a Walk* (Orchard, 1988) and *Two Barks* (Bloodaxe Books, 1998). She received the Michael Hartnett Poetry Award in 2001.

Bernard O'Donoghue was born in Cullen, County Cork in 1945 and still lives there for part of the year. His most recent book of poems, *Here Nor There*, was published by Chatto & Windus in 1999. He is the editor of *Oxford Irish Quotations* (1999), and he teaches Medieval English at Wadham College, Oxford.

Dennis O'Driscoll was born in Thurles, County Tipperary in 1954. His fifth collection of poems, *Weather Permitting* (Anvil Press, 1999), was a Poetry Book Society Recommendation and was shortlisted for the Irish Times Prize for Poetry 2001. His latest publication is *Troubled Thoughts, Majestic Dreams: Selected Prose Writings* (Gallery Books, 2001). He received a Lannan Literary Award in 1999.

Frank Ormsby was born in 1947. He is Head of English at Royal Belfast Academical Institution. His most recent collection of poems is *The Ghost Train* (Gallery, 1995) and he is editor of *The Hip Flask: Short Poems From Ireland*, published recently by Blackstaff Press.

Ruth Padel lives in London and has won the UK National Poetry Prize; *Rembrandt Would Have Loved You* was shortlisted for the T.S. Eliot Prize; her new collection *Voodoo Shop* is a Poetry Book Society Recommendation. She used to teach Classics and is author of *I'm a Man* (Faber), a study in Greek myth, rock music and modern masculinity; she invented the *Independent on Sunday*'s popular 'Sunday Poem' column and wrote it for three years. A selection from it, *52 Ways of Looking at a Poem or How Reading Modern Poetry Can Change Your Life*, appears in June 2002 (Chatto) with an introductory essay, 'Reading Poetry Today'. She is a Fellow of the Society of Authors.

Tom Paulin was born in Leeds in 1949, grew up in Belfast, and was educated at Hull and Oxford Universities. He has published six volumes of poetry as well as *Selected Poems 1972–1990* (Faber, 1993), two major anthologies, versions of Greek drama, and several critical works. He is the E. M. Young Lecturer in English at Hertford College, Oxford. His latest poetry publication – *The Invasion Handbook* – has just appeared from Faber.

Adrian Rice was born in Whitehouse, County Antrim, in 1958. His first sequence of poems appeared in *Muck Island* (1990), a collaboration with Ulster artist, Ross Wilson. Copies of this limited edition box-set are housed in the collections of The Tate Gallery, The Boston Museum of Fine Arts and The Lamont Library, Harvard University. His second poetry sequence was *Impediments* (Abbey Press, 1997). He edited *Signals* (Abbey Press, 1997), an anthology of poetry and prose, and has also edited three anthologies of children's poetry and art. In 1997, he received the Sir James Kilfedder Memorial Bursary for Emerging Artists. In autumn 1999, as recipient of the US/Ireland Residency Exchange Bursary, he was Poet-in-Residence at Lenoir-Rhyne College, North Carolina. His first full poetry collection – *The Mason's Tongue* (Abbey Press, 1999) – was shortlisted for the 2001 Christopher Ewart-Biggs Memorial Literary Prize and was nominated for the 2001 Irish Times Prize for Poetry.

Carol Rumens has published eleven collections of poetry, including *Thinking of Skins* (Bloodaxe, 1993), *Best China Sky* (1995) and *Holding Pattern* (Blackstaff, 1999). The latter was shortlisted for the 1999 Belfast City Arts Award. Her poems appear in several anthologies, including *The Penguin Book of Poetry from Britain and Ireland since 1945* (Eds. Armitage and Crawford) and *The Firebox* (Ed. Sean O'Brien). With her partner, Yuri Drobyshev, she has translated Russian poetry, including work by Pushkin and Yevgeny Rein. She has also published a novel and various short stories, and her literary journalism has appeared in a variety of publications. She has held several writing residencies. From 1991–3, she was Poet-in-Residence at Queen's University, Belfast: she was subsequently instrumental in establishing the new Creative Writing module, in which she participated for several years. She now teaches Creative Writing at the University of Bangor, Wales.

Mark Roper lives in Tobernabrone, County Kilkenny. His first collection, *The Hen Ark* (Peterloo/Salmon, 1990), won the Aldeburgh Poetry Festival Prize in 1991. He has since published *Catching The Light* (Peterloo, 1997), and a chapbook, *The Home Fire* (Abbey Press, 1998). He was Editor of *Poetry Ireland* for 1999.

Frank Sewell is a research officer at the University of Ulster, Coleraine. His poems have previously been published in *Outside the Walls* by Frank Sewell and Francis O'Hare (Belfast: An Clochan, 1997), and in many journals and newspapers. Also a translator, his English language versions of poems in Irish by Cathal Ó Searcaigh, published in *Out in the Open* (Indreabhan: Clo Iar-Chonnachta, 1997), were nominated for the Aristeion European Translation Prize. He co-edited the anthology and touring exhibition *Artwords: an Ulster anthology of contemporary visual art and poetry* (Cranagh Press, 2001). He received the University of Ulster McCrea Literary Award for poetry in 1996 and Literature Awards from the NI Arts Council in 1999 and 2001. His critical work includes *Modern Irish Poetry: A New Alhambra* (OUP, 2000); *Where the Paradoxed Grow*, the Poetry of Derek Mahon (Cranagh Press, 2000); and *On the side of light*, Critical Essays on the Poetry of Cathal Ó Searcaigh, ed. by Frank Sewell and James Doan, forthcoming.

Peter Sirr was born in Waterford in 1960. In 1982, he won the Patrick Kavanagh Award and, in 1998, the O'Shaughnessy Award of the University of St. Thomas Center for Irish Studies. He has published five collections of poetry with Gallery Press: *Marginal Zones* (1984), *Talk, Talk* (1987), *Ways of Falling* (1991), *The Ledger of Fruitful Exchange* (1995) and *Bring Everything* (2000). He currently lives in Dublin where he is Director of the Irish Writers' Centre.

Kevin Smith was born in 1963. He grew up in County Down and graduated from Queen's University, Belfast in 1986. He left Northern Ireland in 1992 to work as a journalist in Eastern Europe, and for the past four years has lived in Dublin. His poems have appeared in numerous periodicals, been broadcast by the BBC, and featured in *The New Younger Irish Poets* (Blackstaff Press).

Matthew Sweeney has recently published *A Smell of Fish* (Cape, 2000). Cape also published *The Bridal Suite* in 1997, and a selection of his earlier work is in *Penguin Modern Poets 12* (1997). Two books of poems for children, *The Flying Spring Onion* (1992) and *Fatso in the Red Suit* (1995), and a novel for children, *The Snow Vulture* (1992), were all published by Faber. *Up on the Roof*, New and Selected poems for children appeared from Faber in 2001. He was editor of *The New Faber Book of Children's Verse* (2001) and co-editor, with Jo Shapcott, of *Emergency Kit: Poems for Strange Times* (Faber, 1996); with Ken Smith, of *Beyond Bedlam: Poems Written Out of Mental Distress* (Anvil, 1997) and co-author, with John Hartley-Williams, of *Writing Poetry* (Hodder & Stoughton, 1997). He received a 1999 Arts Council of England Writers' Award.

David Wheatley is a poet and critic. He has published two collections of poetry, *Thirst* (1997) and *Misery Hill* (2000, both from Gallery Press). He co-edits the poetry journal *Metre* with Justin Quinn and lectures in English at the University of Hull.

Enda Wyley was born in Dublin in 1966. She has published two collections of poetry – *Eating Baby Jesus* in 1994 and *Socrates in the Garden* in 1998 – both by Dedalus Press. She received the Vincent Buckley Memorial Award for Poetry. She has been the recipient of two Arts Council Bursaries for Literature, in 1996 and 2001. She is working on her third collection of poetry, *Diary of a Fat Man*, and a novel. A children's story is forthcoming from O'Brien Press in 2002.

NOTES ON ARTWORKS AND ARTISTS

16
On Through the Silent Lands (1951)   **Jack Butler Yeats** 1871–1957
Oil on canvas

The most distinguished Irish painter of this century, Yeats was the youngest of five children of the painter John Butler Yeats and brother of the poet W. B. Yeats. When he was eight, he was taken to live with his mother's parents in Sligo where much of his imagery was formed. His mature work is an idiosyncratic form of expressionism, having some similarity to the work of Lovis Corinth, but with a strong literary dependency.

18
The Potato Digger (1912–15)   **Paul Henry** 1876–1958
Oil on canvas

One of the most successful painters to have come from Belfast, Henry lived in London between 1900 and 1912. In 1910 he first visited Achill Island, County Mayo, which was to become his favourite painting ground. Here he found the peasant culture he came to celebrate so much. This single figure, painted in Achill before 1915, conveys a sense of pathos he rarely matched.

20
Bewley's Restaurant II (1980)   **Hector McDonnell** b.1947
Oil on canvas

One of the McDonnell family of Glenarm Castle, Hector McDonnell has acquired an international reputation for his painting. The restaurant featured here is a well-known establishment in Dublin. In this large painting, McDonnell has treated the dark interior with light penetrating the windows in the face of the viewer in a novel way, which recalls the paintings of the 'Glasgow Boys' at the turn of the century.

22
Yellow Device (1962)   **Patrick Scott** b. 1921
Tempera on canvas

Patrick Scott studied architecture at University College, Dublin, and has continued to practise it as well as painting. He was one of Ireland's first major abstract painters and has also designed tapestries.

24
The Road to the West (1944) **John Luke** 1906–75
Oil and tempera on board

This was painted when Luke was living with his mother in County Armagh, having left Belfast as a result of the German air raids on the city. The composition was based on an earlier drawing of Slievemore, the mountain which dominates the landscape of Achill Island in the west of Ireland. The title conjures up the romance of the west which has been so important a part of the popular perception of the area. Luke's highly stylized treatment of the landscape contrasts with the more evocative renderings of the same area by his contemporaries.

26
Yellow Bungalow (1954) **Gerard Dillon** 1916–71
Oil on canvas

Dillon was one of the most imaginative of the folk-inspired Irish painters of the 20th century. The youngest of eight children, he left school at fourteen to work as a house-painter and, although his mother enrolled him for evening art classes, he did not attend. He began painting seriously around 1936, visiting Connemara frequently. This picture was painted in a bungalow at Roundstone, County Galway.

28
View of Pont Aven (1899) **Roderic O'Conor** 1860–1940
Oil on canvas

This is one of the most remarkable post-Impressionist landscapes painted by an Irish artist who lived mostly in France. A person of private means, he moved to Brittany, where Gauguin and Van Gogh worked. The influence of both can be seen in this picture, particularly in the bright greens and reds of the landscape and the juxtaposition of strokes of pure blues and greens in the sky. O'Conor was a reclusive figure who, because of his financial independence, could concentrate completely on the kind of painting he felt to be important, without any need to produce work for sale.

32
Riveting **William Conor** 1881–1968
Crayon on paper

It is not certain whether or not this shipyard scene was part of Conor's wartime record of activity in Belfast. It may well have been drawn in the 1930s, when Belfast's shipyards were second to none in the world. Welders and riveters performed highly-skilled and heavy work and were regarded as the 'aristocracy' of the working class. Conor has made a bold compositional contrast between the smooth side of the ship under construction and the intricacy of the hammerhead cranes beyond.

34
Give Me to Drink (1949)   **Colin Middleton** 1910–83
Oil on canvas

The Dublin art dealer Victor Waddington became interested in Middleton's work after the artist's return to Belfast in 1948. Middleton was given his first London one-man show in 1952, in which this painting was included. One of a series of contemporary pictures with biblical themes, painted with an expressionist brushstroke, it shows the conversation between Jesus and the Samaritan woman at the well. The exaggeratedly Semitic types reflect Middleton's deep concern at this time for the Nazi holocaust and the plight of Jewish refugees in Europe.

36
Slan Leat a Athair/Goodbye, Father (1935)   **Séan Keating** 1889–1977
Oil on canvas

At the time of the founding of the Irish Free State in the 1920s, Keating, who taught at the Dublin Municipal School of Art, was the country's leading abstract painter. His subject matter was self-consciously patriotic and nationalist, as in this scene where the Aran Islanders bid their priest farewell as he departs in a curragh.

38
Eileen, Her First Communion (1901)   **Sir John Lavery** 1856–1941
Oil on board

Born in Belfast, Lavery attained the highest position in London as a society portrait painter, helped admittedly by his beautiful American second wife, Hazel. This work was painted earlier, showing his daughter by his first marriage, in her communion dress.

40
Farm in Winter (1966)   **Tony O'Malley** b.1913
Gouache and acrylic on paper

The artist wrote in 1978: "This was painted from drawings made in previous months around the Cornish coast and from earlier drawings of coastal farms in County Wexford. My experience of such farmsteads enabled me to express in this gouache the winter atmosphere and the huddle of the farm buildings under the hill with the stormy sea's horizon as a backdrop". Official recognition in Ireland for O'Malley's work did not come until 1975, but he is now one of the most revered of Irish painters.

42

Mr. and Mrs. Stanley Joscelyne: The Second Marriage (1972)
Anthony Green *b.*1939
Oil on board

Most of Green's work is to do with members of his own family, with relationships between them, their hopes, fears and aspirations. Often his compositions quote from old master paintings, as here, where the subject matter itself – marriage – the mirror in the background and the chandelier overhead recall Van Eyck's famous *Marriage of Arnolfini*. The interior is that of Green's parents' home in north London.

44

Ecclesiastical Ruins on Inniscaltra, or Holy Island, Lough Derg, Co.
Galway, after Sunset: "This Island is One of Great Historic Interest ..."
– Petrie (c.1863)
Bartholomew Colles Watkins 1833–91
Oil on canvas

Colles Watkins devoted himself to painting Irish landscape in a particularly detailed style and places like Connemara and Killarney featured among his favourite sites. As he worked slowly, his pictures are not plentiful. This is a very good example showing Irish monastic ruins against an evocative sunset.

48

Five Trees by a River   **Hans Iten** 1874–1930
Oil on canvas on panel

Born in Switzerland, Hans Iten studied in his native country and in Paris before coming to Belfast as a damask designer in 1904. He spent most of his working life in the city. This little panel, which may have been painted on the banks of the Lagan, is a good example of Iten's broad impressionistic style.

50

Eventide   **George William 'Æ' Russell** 1867–1935
Oil on canvas

The 'myriad-minded' polymath George Russell was painter, poet, economist and mystic. This evocative evening scene with its sickle moon appears to be set in the west of Ireland, which Russell described as "charged with energy". It is, however, an entirely objective picture, with a pre-Raphaelite melancholy atmosphere. Perhaps it is significant that this preoccupation with creating moods should be the work of a painter who also expressed his feelings as a poet and writer.

52
Big Tench Lake (1972)   **Barrie Cooke** *b*.1931
Oil on two canvases, with a perspex box

Brought up in the Caribbean and educated at Harvard, Barrie Cooke settled in Ireland in 1954. He is renowned for his paintings of rivers and water, and is an expert angler.

54
Girl in White (1941)   **Louis le Brocquy** *b*.1916
Oil on canvas on board

Born in Dublin of Belgian parentage, le Brocquy is probably the most internationally distinguished living Irish artist. This early portrait shows much influence from the profile portraits of Whistler, with their oriental accessories.

56
Inside No. 3 (1979)   **Robert Ballagh** *b*.1943
Acrylic on canvas

This painting takes its name from Ballagh's small Dublin house. Originally trained as an architect, he designed the interior himself. Ballagh's wife descends the spiral staircase, while the artist's face appears on the television screen.

58
Field of Corn, Pont Aven (1892)   **Roderic O'Conor** 1860–1940
Oil on canvas

Coming from a comfortable landowning background, Roderic O'Conor enjoyed financial independence which enabled him to settle in France as a young man and to concentrate on painting without economic pressures. He was a member of the circle of post-Impressionist painters who congregated around Paul Gauguin in the Breton village of Pont-Aven, where this remarkable little picture was painted. The juxtapositioning of complementary colours reminds us of the work of Van Gogh, who was dead by the time this was painted.

60
John Montague b.1929 (1983)   **Edward McGuire** 1932–86
Oil on panel

Edward McGuire painted many portraits of literary figures and this one of the Tyrone-born poet is one of three in the Museum's collection, the others being of Seamus Heaney and Francis Stuart.

64
Children Playing on Lagan   **Gerard Dillon** 1916–71
Oil on canvas on cardboard

Dillon worked for a decorating firm in London in the late 1930s and began painting seriously about 1936, frequently visiting Connemara. He spent the war years in Belfast and Dublin and was associated with George Campbell and Dan O'Neill. Dillon's subject matter revolves around his experiences growing up on the Falls Road in Belfast, in working class terraced houses. This early painting shares its subject matter with much of the work of another Belfast artist, William Conor.

66
Ghost of a Place (1981)   **Tony O'Malley** *b.*1913
Oil on board

A member of the St Ives School of painters, O'Malley is one of Ireland's finest painters. All his work originates in nature and the atmosphere of places. He divided his time between the Bahamas, Cornwall and Ireland until the late 1980s and then spent winters in Lanzarote before moving permanently to Ireland in 1990.

68
The Fun of the Fair (1908)   **A. Romilly Fedden** 1875–1939
Watercolour on paper

Fedden was a disciple of Arthur Melville, who advocated the 'wet method' of watercolour painting. This entails completely soaking the paper and carefully dripping the paint in blobs. Great skill is required to avoid creating a formless mess. This fair in Oxfordshire is an unusual subject for a watercolour.

70
Daylight Raid from my Studio Window, 7 July 1917
Sir John Lavery 1856–1941
Oil on canvas

The setting for this painting is Lavery's studio in Kensington, London. He moved into the studio in 1899, when he first established his reputation as a fashionable painter. The figure is his wife, Hazel, and she is seen looking out of the window at the air raid which took place on the morning of 7 July 1917, only the second such raid to have occurred over London by that date. Lavery's execution of the picture has been brisk and spontaneous, yet the deft brushwork brilliantly catches the light and the varied contents of the interior, and conveys a good idea of the atmosphere in his studio.

72
Passion Bed (1990)   **Dorothy Cross** *b.*1956
Sculpture, wire and sand-blasted wine glasses

Now one of Ireland's most acclaimed sculptors of the younger generation, Dorothy Cross works in a wide variety of materials, including cows' udders. This work uses a wire framework holding pierced and engraved wine glasses.

74
Head (1938)   **Colin Middleton** 1910–83
Oil on board

Middleton discovered the work of Salvador Dali and the Belgian surrealists in the mid-1930s and this was to him an eye-opener. Surrealism was to be a recurring factor in his own paintings for the rest of his life, although he himself preferred the term 'superrealism'. This jewel-like little painting is significant in that it seems to be the earliest surrealist painting by an Irish artist – it pre-dates by several years the White Stag group of Dublin painters who drew heavily on Freudian psychology and surrealism during the Irish Free State's wartime neutrality.

76
The Watcher   **George William 'Æ' Russell** 1867–1935
Oil on canvas

This extensive landscape of an Irish bog may be read on two levels. The figure could be flesh-and-blood or a brooding elemental, one of the sibh, beings which the visionary Russell claimed to see frequently. The sunlight breaking through the clouds reflected in the watery pool recalls some of the paintings of Paul Henry. Russell's landscape paintings have tended to be under-rated, whereas he was most skilful in rendering the damp-laden atmosphere of the west of Ireland.

78
Dawn, Killary Harbour (*c.*1921)   **Paul Henry** 1876–1958
Oil on canvas

One of the most successful painters to have come from Belfast, Paul Henry studied in Paris and lived in London in the early years of the 20th century, where he was much influenced by Whistler and the post-Impressionists. He made frequent visits to Ireland, particularly the west, and first visited Achill Island, County Mayo, in 1910. Probably unknowingly, he suffered from red-green colour blindness, which accounts for the restricted palette of this beautiful landscape of western Mayo.

80
Rustics Dancing outside an Inn   **Sampson Towgood Roch(e)** 1757/59–1847
Watercolour on paper

Like so many miniature painters, Roch(e) was born a deaf-mute. He married his first cousin, who brought him a handsome fortune, and in 1792 moved to Bath, where he carried on a successful practice until retirement brought him back to County Waterford. This work is a fancy subject, the inn and the church in the background evidently imaginary, and the 'rustics' very genteel. As might be expected from a painter of miniatures, the strokes are tiny and white bodycolour is used as well as watercolour.

82
Tired Child (1954)   **Louis le Brocquy** *b*.1916
Oil on Canvas

Of Belgian extraction, Louis le Brocquy is probably the most internationally regarded living Irish painter. He abandoned a career as a chemist to become a painter, and lived for a long period in the south of France. He now lives in Dublin. This is a middle period painting in which the technique used is a form of cubism.

84
The Three Dancers (1945)   **John Luke** 1906–75
Oil and tempera on canvas on board

Luke himself described this painting as "an interesting piece of craftsmanship … [in it] I have practically reached the limit of my knowledge". It was painted while he was living in County Armagh and is one of the first of a number of almost visionary compositions which he produced in the mid-1940s.

86
Dream of the Moth (1976–77)   **Colin Middleton** 1910–83
Oil on board

Unlike many artists, Middleton was most articulate in describing the significance of his paintings. This one belongs to a cycle called Transformations, Metamorphoses and Visitations, stemming from his discovery of a linden leaf in a Fermanagh forest. He took the leaf back to his studio and for a period "it virtually took over". Middleton's work has been described as surrealist, although the artist himself preferred the word 'superrealism', in which he included himself with "such kindred souls as Bosch, Blake and others".

88

The Potato Gatherers **George William 'Æ' Russell** 1867–1935
Oil on canvas

This painting formerly belonged to Lily Yeats, sister of the poet W. B. Yeats and the painter Jack Butler Yeats. It shows 'Æ' using a broadly painted objective style deriving from the 'peasantries' of the French painter Jean-Claude Millet. His work was also influenced by the young Paul Henry and one may be forgiven for mistaking this painting for one of Henry's.

90

Shapes and Shadows (1962) **William Scott** 1913–89
Oil on canvas

Brought up in Enniskillen, William Scott became the most internationally renowned painter to emerge from Northern Ireland in the 20th century. Originally broadly representational, his paintings gradually became more abstract, but never lost their reference to landscape tonality.

94

The Green Coat (1926) **Sir John Lavery** 1856–1941
Oil on canvas

Lavery is undoubtedly the most distinguished artist to have emerged from Belfast. His beautiful American second wife, Hazel, is the subject of this portrait. Contemporary illustrations show that the painting was originally shown without the green coat. To add the coat, Lavery moved his wife's left hand and painted out a satin cushion on the right of the picture.

96

Village by the Sea (1953) **Norah McGuinness** 1901–80
Oil on canvas

Daughter of a Derry coal merchant and ship owner, Norah McGuinness studied in Dublin, and in Paris under Andre Lhote, although his frigid academic cubism failed to influence her. After a period in America, she returned to Ireland permanently in 1939. Her work at this time was inspired by the French Fauves of thirty years before. This work was painted in the harbour village of Dunmore East, County Waterford.

98

Dublin Street Scene No. 1 (1947–48) **Edward Burra** 1905–76
Pencil and watercolour on paper

The fact that Burra's health was always delicate has been taken to explain why he worked largely in watercolour and why he spent most of his life in seclusion at the family home in Rye, but it did not prevent him from travelling a great deal in Europe, the United States and Mexico in search of the steamy street life which fascinated him and contrasted with his own bourgeois background. He visited Ireland several times in the late 1940s and liked the decaying Georgian terraces of Dublin. His painting had stagnated since about 1942, but the material he found in Ireland re-invigorated it and unlike many artists he did not idealise Irish 'peasantry'.

100
Boon Companions (1934) **Harry Kernoff** 1900–74
Pencil and watercolour on paper

The son of a Russian-Jewish furniture-maker and a Spanish mother, Harry Kernoff was brought to Dublin when the family moved there in 1914. Davy Byrne's was, and still is, a well-known literary pub off Grafton Street, Dublin. This painting shows the back snug, where favoured drinkers were invited as guests of the landlord, Davy Byrne, who appears in the centre. Kernoff himself is on the left and the third figure is Martin Murphy, a stage carpenter at the Gate Theatre, for which Kernoff designed sets.

102
Fête Day in a Cider Orchard, Normandy (1878)
William John Hennessy 1839–1917
Oil on canvas

Born in Kilkenny and trained in New York, Hennessy moved to London in 1870 and from 1875 spent part of each year in Brittany and Normandy. This was painted in 1878 and shows Norman peasants playing quilles, a rustic form of skittles.

106
Negative (4) (1994) **Mark Francis** *b.*1962
Oil on canvas

Mark Francis was born in County Down and trained in London. One of a series of paintings, this work was donated to the Ulster Museum in 1996. Another in the series can be seen in the Hugh Lane Gallery in Dublin.

108
Huckleberry Finn (1885) **Aloysius O'Kelly** 1850–1929
Oil on canvas

O'Kelly became a student in Paris in 1874 and subsequently spent much of his time in Brittany. He left there for America in 1909 and exhibited in New York and Chicago. This painting features one of American writer Mark Twain's best-known characters.

110
The Barn (Blue II) (1991–92) **Basil Blackshaw** *b.*1923
Oil on canvas

Now possibly Northern Ireland's most distinguished living painter, Blackshaw lives and works in the country near Antrim, finding much material in the world of dog handling. This was painted in 1991–92, showing the broadness of handling in Blackshaw's mature style.

112
The Fox (1937) **John Luke** 1906–75
Oil and tempera on panel

After leaving the Slade School of Art in 1931, John Luke developed the careful drawing style he had learnt there under Henry Tonks into his own distinctive tempera technique. In provincial Belfast, this was considered startlingly modern. This work is a landscape of the imagination, the colours of which are not based on nature. Like most of Luke's mature paintings, the picture was painstakingly built up in layers of thin water-based tempera paint. For many years, Luke taught life classes at Belfast College of Art and he was revered by generations of students for his obsessional exactitude and concentration.

114
Scene in Co. Wicklow (1820) **James Arthur O'Connor** 1792–1841
Oil on canvas

After 1822, O'Connor settled in London, exhibiting at the Royal Academy and the British Institution. This work is an idealised view of the Wicklow countryside in the tradition of classical landscape painting, with the mountains Italianised in treatment in the manner of the great 17th century painter Claude Lorraine. Later on, O'Connor's landscapes became much more gloomy and melancholic, in accord with contemporary tastes for the sublime or romantic.

116
Lagan: Annadale, October (1941) **Colin Middleton** 1910–1983
Oil on canvas

This was the first of Middleton's paintings to enter a public collection, bought by the Belfast Museum and Art Gallery in 1943. At the outbreak of war, the art galleries at Stranmillis were stripped and the collections sent out of town. A one-man show of one hundred and fifteen works by Middleton, including this painting, was organised in the empty galleries in 1943. The Belfast public was astonished by the variety of work by one man and the artist Tom Carr described the exhibition as "an amazing anthology of modern art".

118
Egypt Series No. 3 (1972) **William Scott** 1913–89
Oil on canvas

William Scott's art, whether on an intimate or monumental scale, moves from the objective to the abstract. In 1955, he visited the Lascaux caves and in 1970, he went to Egypt. The art of both cultures impressed him by its anonymity. This large painting dates from 1972, after the visit to Egypt.

120
The End of the World (1909) **Jack Butler Yeats** 1871–1957
Pencil, ink and watercolour on paper

Between 1888 and 1910, Jack Yeats worked as a professional illustrator for many papers and this humorous illustration was published in a magazine, *The Broadside*, in 1909. It was seen by Yeats's friend, the poet John Masefield, who wrote to him that year, " … Let me tell you how much I enjoyed your picture of 'The End of the World'. That was one of the best of all your drawings. I liked to think that the two gentlemen making for the tree were you and I".

122
Three Friends (1969–70) **Daniel O'Neill** 1920–74
Oil on board

Dan O'Neill had hardly any formal training as a painter and until 1944 he worked as an electrical engineer in the Belfast shipyards and painted only in his spare time. He then received encouragement from collectors and critics and was given one-man shows by Victor Waddington's gallery. He is often associated with two other primitive artists, Gerard Dillon and George Campbell. This is one of three late paintings exhibited in 1971.

124
Self-contained Flat (*c.*1953) **Gerard Dillon** 1916–1971
Oil on hardboard

From 1945 to 1968, Gerard Dillon lived mostly in London, where this was painted almost as a manifesto-picture. He found the freedom and anonymity of London a relaxation from the narrow bigotry of his west Belfast youth and the self-contained flat a symbol of this independence. He has shown himself three times, returning from work, cultivating his garden and, in the foreground, posing proudly with the tools of his trade as a housepainter.

ACKNOWLEDGEMENTS

The editors and publishers wish to thank the following for permission to reproduce artworks in copyright:

Robert Ballagh, © Robert Ballagh; **Basil Blackshaw,** © Basil Blackshaw; **Edward Burra,** Care of Alex Reid and Lefevre, London; **William Conor,** © Estate of William Conor; **Barrie Cooke,** © Barrie Cooke; **Dorothy Cross,** © Care of Kerlin Gallery, Dublin; **Gerard Dillon,** © Gerard Dillon; **A. Romilly Fedden,** © Ms Frances Fedden; **Mark Francis,** © Mark Francis; **Anthony Green,** © Anthony Green; **Séan Keating,** © Estate of Séan Keating; **Harry Kernoff,** © Ms Catriona Kernoff; **Sir John Lavery,** © Estate of Sir John Lavery/Felix Rosenstiel's Widow & Son Limited; **Louis le Brocquy,** © Louis le Brocquy; **John Luke,** © Mrs Sarah McKee; **Hector McDonnell,** © Hector McDonnell; **Norah McGuinness,** © Miss Rhoda McGuinness; **Edward McGuire,** © By kind permission of Mrs Sally McGuire; **Colin Middleton,** © Ms Jane Middleton Giddens; **Roderic O'Conor,** © Sister Theophane Dwyer; **Tony O'Malley,** © Tony O'Malley; **Daniel O'Neill,** © Mrs Patricia Forster; **George William Russell ('Æ'),** © 2002, reprinted by the permission of Russell & Volkening as agents for the Estate of George William Russell; **Patrick Scott,** © Patrick Scott; **William Scott,** © William Scott Estate; **Jack Butler Yeats,** © Michael Yeats.

The editors and publishers also gratefully acknowledge permission to include the following poems in copyright:

Peter Fallon, 'A Thanksgiving', by kind permission of the author, Loughcrew, Oldcastle, Co. Meath, Ireland; Seamus Heaney, 'The Guttural Muse' from *Field Work* (Faber & Faber, 1979), by permission of Faber & Faber; from *Opened Ground: Selected Poems 1966 – 1996* by Seamus Heaney. Copyright © 1998 by Seamus Heaney. Reprinted by permission of Farrar, Straus and Giroux, LLC; Derek Mahon, 'Shapes and Shadows' from *Collected Poems* (1999), by kind permission of the author and The Gallery Press, Loughcrew, Oldcastle, Co. Meath, Ireland; John Montague, 'The Yachtsman's Jacket' from *Smashing the Piano* (1999), by kind permission of the author and The Gallery Press; Tom Paulin, 'On' (extract) from *Walking a Line* (Faber & Faber, 1994), by permission of Faber & Faber; Adrian Rice, 'The Mason's Tongue' from *The Mason's Tongue* (Abbey Press, 1999), by permission of Abbey Press.